AFFIRM
Greatness
REALIZE
Destiny

MOTIVATING MEMOIRS TO ENCOURAGE & EMPOWER

CONSUELO GAINES

AFFIRM GREATNESS - REALIZE DESTINY
Motivating Memoirs To Encourage & Empower

Consuelo Gaines
cgaineskdg@gmail.com

ISBN 978-1-949826-31-9

Printed in the USA.
All rights reserved

Published by: EAGLES GLOBAL BOOKS | Frisco, Texas
In conjunction with the 2021 Eagles Authors Course
Cover & interior designed by DestinedToPublish.com

ENDORSEMENTS

With confidence and joy, *Affirm Greatness, Realize Destiny* is a great collection of devotionals to help us realize that we are who God called us to be. The world may try to label you one way, but the truth is that you are a unique masterpiece. The various affirmations are uplifting and filled with scriptural guidance to lead us to our own journey of knowing "I am who God says I am." This book inspires hope and allows readers to reevaluate their lives. We are grateful to God that Gaines has shared these memoirs to help set the course and shape your future.

Apostle Eric and Pastor Lisa Harris
Senior Pastors of Temple of Deliverance LCM, Chicago

. . . .

This book will indeed provoke a greater level of understanding and foster maturity in the Christian walk of faith.

Dr. Kina N. Arnold

DEDICATION

To Faithful Father God, without Whom nothing I am or do is possible; to my natural and faith families with great love and affection for the seeds you have sown into me, for the lessons you have taught me, and for the patience you have demonstrated; and to all those stewarded to me, whom it is my honor and pleasure to serve.

ACKNOWLEDGMENTS

To my first teacher, instructor, and encourager, Mommy, and to all those who followed. You all, by God's grace, imparted teaching, instruction, encouragement, and correction. I cannot thank God enough for you! You have my eternal love, admiration, and appreciation. Multiplied blessings of agape and shalom to you all.

FOREWORD

*"God told me to **write** down in **a book** words meant for the coming generation as an eternal witness."* (Isaiah 30:8 TPT)

*"**One generation after another** will celebrate Your great works; they **will pass on the story of Your powerful acts to their children**. Your majesty and glorious splendor have captivated me; I will meditate on Your wonders, sing songs of Your worth."* (Psalm 145:4-5 VOICE)

When I was in the fourth grade, I wrote my very first "book." It was a child's creatively self-illustrated short story about the adventures of a ladybug. That was the beginning – since that time, God has allowed me to author several books and to found Tryuni Publications. The words and messages in the books have inspired, encouraged, trained, equipped, comforted, and invigorated generations of readers and leaders.

I am an author, attorney, and international instructor, among many other things. Through these capacities, I had the privilege of meeting and working with Consuelo Gaines. There are many noteworthy truths that become evident when you are blessed to meet and work with Consuelo Gaines. Two of the most important are: 1) she is a true reflection of her Heavenly Father, and 2) she lives according to the principles of the Kingdom of God. Consuelo is a Kingdom educator and uses her skills to positively impact various spheres of influence.

Some of these skills, like the love of reading, writing, and communicating, can begin with a small seed that grows and develops over time. Consuelo Gaines's words in *Motivating Memoirs* begin with the seeds of her life. In this book, Consuelo follows the patterns and examples of Jesus Christ, her beloved Savior. Jesus was obedient to the voice of Father God; thus, Jesus fulfilled His purpose in the earth. His life impacted all of creation for all eternity.

During His earthly ministry, Jesus often taught the people using parables, and He would frequently introduce a topic by referring to a passage of Scripture. He presented engaging parables that confronted personal or societal issues of the day. He posed rhetorical questions that challenged the status quo and stimulated the spirit, soul, heart, emotions, and intellect of the listener. He challenged the listener to reflect on their personal behavior, reconsider their spiritual aptitude and respond differently to societal issues, and change their spiritual condition. Jesus used the parables to elaborate on the principles of the Kingdom of God. He provided guidance on how to apply Kingdom principles to overcome earthly issues. Jesus is the living Word who came to the earth to help all generations of mankind learn about the love of God and provide instructions for entering the more excellent ways of His Heavenly Father's Kingdom.

Motivating Memoirs by Consuelo Gaines does the same. God spoke and she obeyed. You are holding this book in your hands and reading these words because Consuelo Gaines obeyed the voice of the LORD to write this book. *Motivating Memoirs* contains words that serve as an eternal witness to generations of people.

Consuelo Gaines has written a book that utilizes the memoirs of her life to motivate, educate, challenge, and inspire. Her perspective on life and observations regarding the sovereign plans of God are captured in her dynamic collection of memories, poignant experiences, and precious moments from her life that have left indelible marks on her destiny. She masterfully uses personal accounts – sometimes funny, oftentimes poignant stories from her life.

Each chapter begins with the Words of GOD and a riveting personal memoir. Ultimately, I believe that God is using Consuelo's transparency to invite us to reconsider the memoirs of our lives and examine them for the handprint of God. She lovingly, yet thoroughly strips away excuses, artificial limitations, and blatant fabrications for why we cannot achieve, why we cannot overcome and be who God originally created and envisions us to be.

Consuelo challenges the status quo and the mediocrity mindset. She demonstrates how readers can stop accepting artificial limitations. The chapters contain questions for self-examination and personal reflections. The Power Points and Affirmations sections provide tools, strategies, practical pointers, and motivation to conquer life's challenges. Consuelo shows us that we too can overcome stigmas and stereotypes.

If you have tended to look at life as "a glass half empty rather than half full," prepare for a shift in your outlook. *Motivating Memoirs* will encourage you to see your life as full and overflowing. It inspires you to reexamine what and how you think about your origins and life circumstances from your past, as well as your purposes in the present and possibilities for the future.

Every page of *Motivating Memoirs* testifies and demonstrates how Consuelo Gaines is an authentic living and walking example of Romans 8:28 (AMP): "*And we know [with great confidence] that God [who is deeply concerned about us] causes all things to work together [as a plan] for good for those who love God, to those who are called according to His plan and purpose.*"

In Consuelo's own words:

"AMEN!

I am not an underachiever, I am an overcomer, no average mindset nor conformity. I elevate my thinking and innovate!

I live in revelation, faith, and liberty!

I extract the greatness inside of me – the Anointing Oil!

I think bigger, I think better, I live better, I cause and inspire others to do so as well!

I am not mediocre. I am an EXTRAORDINARY EXPRESSION of Faithful Father God with the UNLIMITED capacity for the MORE!"

Are you ready to begin gathering and creating your own Motivating Memoirs? Turn the page and let your new perspective on life begin. When you finish *Motivating Memoirs*, you will be confidently declaring the same motivating affirmations over your life that Consuelo Gaines declares: "I am not mediocre. I am an EXTRAORDINARY EXPRESSION of Faithful Father God with the UNLIMITED capacity for the MORE!!!"

God Bless You,

Apostle Dr. Cynthia Dempsey.

Ph.D. Christian Education and J.D.
Founder, Tryuni Publications
Founder, Kingdom Come Intellectual Property Protections

CONTENTS

INTRODUCTION

I am often wonderstruck at the God-moments and divine handiwork that I see in life. Initially, I mostly recognized them in hindsight, until I began to build a deep abiding relationship with Father God, through the Son, by Holy Spirit. As with all things divine, this is a faith walk. I now recognize patterns in life that are orchestrated by our Father, just like Jesus teaches. When we build deep, abiding relationship with the Lord, we begin to recognize and identify His character and change our perspective. Often the difference between seeing a situation as positive or negative is a matter of perspective: what we know, believe, and understand will color and affect our responses and reactions.

I know my name. It has been taught to me. I have lived with it. I have deep, abiding relationship with it. Because of those facts, no one can convince me that my name isn't my name. Those facts color my belief and my response and reaction. Similarly, when we build deep, abiding relationship with the Lord and begin to recognize and understand His character, we cannot be swayed or deterred from what we know, understand, and experience. As with ourselves and others we know intimately, we cannot be convinced that their character or actions are something that they are not.

This volume is an invitation. It is an invitation to give you glimpses of my own life, knowledge, understanding, and experiences building this deep, abiding relationship with Father God. I present this invitation so that I might draw you in to desire and cultivate your own deep, abiding relationship. I invite you into a perspective that deviates from what many in the world would call the norm or what is popularly accepted; to see from a different lens, a biblical lens, a lens of Truth and not necessarily facts. May you accept the invitation and be blessed by the journey and the challenge.

Every one of us has gifts, talents, callings, and triumphs that await us. But, too often, the pressures, setbacks, excuses, challenges, and tragedies of life tempt us to give up on our dreams, visions, successes, blessings, and destinies (destinations). This collection chronicles the lessons I have learned about overcoming these life obstacles that may oppose the success and blessing for which we are destined and designed.

The human mind, body, soul, and spirit are made for greatness. They are designed to meet, accept, overcome, and win challenges, turning those challenges into triumphs. Given the right tools and time, the physical body will heal itself. The same is true for the mind, the soul, and the spirit. I present to you these life lessons as tools to aid in healing and success. In these lessons, I offer a hope that decrees we do not have to take facts, opinions, social indoctrinations, or adverse events as the deciding factors of our lives. I present motivators to stir your heart, truths to believe, and affirmations to enact steps on the road of destiny (destination) to the greatness for which you are created. May these motivators, truths, and affirmations launch you into being the best of who you are designed to be.

By the world's standards, I was born and raised in the most "at-risk" and failing of circumstances. I was born to what the world would describe as impoverished, urban, unwed, early-teen parents, both of whom came from sizeable single-parent households. I am the eldest of an inordinate number of siblings and a member of multiple blended families, both maternally and paternally. By all accounts of our societal experts, I should be among the most deprived and deviant of our society, BUT GOD! I happen to be the first of my generation on both sides of my family to complete higher education, own property, and embark on a professional career.

This potential setup for a life of more failures than successes, just surviving rather than thriving, happened to be the lot of many with whom I engaged all along the way, and the aforementioned societal experts would certainly have expected it of me as well. Had I not been introduced to and provided with guidance, tools, and inspiration to counter the negative potential, or had I chosen to give in to the beliefs and expectations of others, no doubt my story would have had a much different outcome. Thankfully, the tools provided to and employed by me (even when I was not keenly aware of it) empowered me to make choices that would create room for a life and destination (destiny) that the world and its experts would scarcely have afforded me.

I share my experiences with you to provide you with similar strategies and perspectives, with hope for a destination that rises above where others may categorize you, launching you into purpose and destiny beyond the limitations of where your birth, culture, circumstances, or social standing may dictate. May you too garner a perspective that causes you to move full speed ahead to the destinations of success, and may you not just survive but thrive!

"...there is nothing new under the sun." (Ecclesiastes 1:9b NKJV)

While the specifics here do not represent everyone's story, God's ultimate plan is as He is – constant. It does not change. It remains the same.

Neither are the strategies of the enemy different. Regardless of the specific ingredients, the results of the recipe are the same. The enemy seeks *"to steal, and to kill, and to destroy"* (John 10:10 NKJV).

This collection is compiled to give combative strategies against the tactics of the enemy. Use it to sharpen the sword of the Spirit, to parry as you gain skill, to polish your shield of faith (Ephesians 6:16-17). This volume is designed to strengthen you to quench the fiery darts that the enemy will hurl at you and the onslaught of offensive weaponry he will send.

Throughout the following pages, I share parts of my story and my journey into learning to use Truth and spiritual principles to stand victorious against the enemy and the world. I share help to thwart their attempts to confine believers to the proverbial box of limitations that tempt one to settle for defeat or for a less-than-victorious life. I share these to aid and assist those needing an example of hope, the hope in us that we may not even recognize

(Colossians 1:27). I share hope to keep us on the path to choices that result in growth, progress, and transformation. I share these excerpts to stir motivation and yield strategy to combat the statistical "norms" of the world. I share these principles so you will actively engage in sowing and nurturing seeds that result in transformed thinking, renewed minds, and timeless, eternal truths that will act as anchors when the storms of life arise and when the statistics of the world are against us.

At the end of each brief life lesson, I have shared power points and affirmations. I invite and encourage you to meditate on the power points and to both personalize and vocalize the affirmations. Words have power! What we speak, we hear. Faith comes by hearing, and hearing, and hearing (Romans 10:17). What we hear often enough, we believe. What we believe, we act upon. What we act upon, we manifest. So, go forth and work the Word. The Word works (Mark 11:23). Speak life (John 6:68)! Transform your thinking, your believing, your speaking, your achieving.

Before The Beginning

Before The Beginning

"Though thy beginning was small, yet thy latter end should greatly increase." (Job 8:7 KJV)

I am not tall in stature, not excessively aesthetically pleasing to the eye, nor do I have dynamic curves and proportions. I am not a fan of bright and bold colors or eye-catching expensive jewels. I am not in tune with the latest trends and fashions. In fact, according to the world standard, I am probably pretty plain-Jane-ish, one who easily blends into the background and never really quite fits in anywhere (really, not even among family). There was a time when this niggled at my ill-placed desire to be "normal" and like everyone else; however, I have since gratefully released that notion altogether. One of the defining moments of that release was hearing my mother tell the story of my birth. I am often amazed at the providence of God and how His orchestration of events and answers is never quite like anyone would expect until we see the bigger picture. The handiwork and providence of God often make much more sense in hindsight.

My mother told me of a little girl whose greatest desire was to be a mother, and to have someone to shower love upon and receive love from in return. She spoke of a young preteen who prayed for the same. Similar to the almost heretical thought of a divine King being born in a barn structure among farm animals lauded by dusty shepherds, no one would have thought anything good could come out of a pair of poor, barely teen, inner-city housing project kids from latchkey homes making a baby. This, however, was my humble beginning. My mother went on to reveal that I was the answer to that little girl's prayer. While the dire circumstances were not to the liking of any involved, nor of their families, that little girl was convinced that her answer came from God. Faced with the ultimatum of giving up the child for which she prayed and carried to healthy term, that forlorn, unwed, barely teen, inner-city housing project latchkey kid returned to the Throne, the only Source she knew, and in desperation prayed to keep her answer. Her prayers were heard and answered. She got to keep her baby and to tell her daughter the circumstances surrounding her motherly gratitude for that daughter's having been born and gifted to her.

Now, I don't assume to compare my birth with that of Jesus (God forbid). However, at a time when I seriously doubted my worth, abilities, importance, and significance, God allowed me to hear how I was the answer to someone's prayer. I was the fulfillment of someone's life dream and goal and vision before I ever knew or could fathom it, before I was even born. That stuck with me.

Who might say the same of you? Whose dream, goal, and vision might you be the answer to, the fulfillment of? Who was waiting for your birth, for you to show up on the scene, before you ever did? Who is to say, whatever your beginning, whatever the circumstances of your birth and your place in society at that time, that it is anything less than the answer that at least one person wanted, needed, or prayed fervently for at that set time? Could it possibly be that the same may be true for more than one person and that God Himself chose you for specific purpose and fulfillment? I believe so! The question was even asked of Jesus Himself: could anything good come out of His neighborhood, His town, His side of the proverbial "tracks" (John 1:46)? Of course, in hindsight, we know the answer is that Jesus was and is Good. But, at the time, that was not necessarily apparent to anyone outside of his earthly parents and a set of cousins (Luke 2). That made it no less true. Jesus was secure in who He was, His purpose, His mission, no matter that others were not. He affirmed Himself in who He was, no matter that others did not. Once we have that same security, we can operate in the same type of confidence in thwarting societal norms and living a life of purposeful success.

Will you believe so? Believe it? Confess it? Affirm it? Know that you have purpose and that, because you are, because you were born, someone will see the fulfillment of their own call, purpose, dream, goal, vision. You matter! You are significant! You are needed! Meditate on that truth, selah, think it, believe it, affirm it (Proverbs 23:7a).

POWER POINT

God says,

"Before I formed thee in the belly I knew thee; and before thou camest forth out of the womb I sanctified thee, and I ordained thee…" (Jeremiah 1:5 KJV)

"Do not despise these small beginnings, for the Lord rejoices to see the work begin…" (Zechariah 4:10 NLT)

AFFIRMATION

God knows me, and He knew me even before my beginning. I matter. I am significant. I am needed. I have purpose. I am confident that I make a difference! I am the answer to someone's heartfelt prayer and longing. I choose to believe that something good has come because God allowed me to be here, in this place, this moment, this time. I purpose to cherish the gift God has made me in the lives of all those He has connected me to.

CHAPTER 1

STATISTICAL ANOMALY

"Who would have believed what we heard? Who saw the Lord's power in this?" (Isaiah 53:1 NCV)

"God will always be proven faithful and true to his word, while people are proven to be liars. This will fulfill what was written in the Scriptures: Your words will always be vindicated and you will rise victorious when you are being tried by your critics!" (Romans 3:4 TPT)

I hail from a community (communities, really) of people classified as minority, urban, impoverished, underprivileged. Those may not be the current politically correct terms, but you get the picture.

By the world's standard, I was a statistic: a little black girl born to a barely teenage latchkey single mother not yet even of legal age. In any community, that was a statistical death sentence. If poverty didn't do me in, crime would. Either of those two were paths carved leading to an endless cycle of teen pregnancy, limited housing opportunity, low income, and poor nutrition. These would ultimately find me either homeless, incarcerated (criminally or mentally), addicted to substance abuse, or succumbing to one of the many medical diseases that often plague poor communities. Statistically speaking, that is.

By the world's standards and statistics, I was beat out of the gate. Truth be told, this was and is the story of many whom I originally knew from my origins, including my own biological father. What I have discovered, however, is that there are two diametrically opposed systems at work in the world. Each individual has the option to choose the system in which to operate. No matter our lot in life, no matter how, where, or to whom we are born, we have the opportunity to choose to believe and accept one of the two systems: God's or the world's. The world's system is rooted in that which opposes God.

As the lives of biblical characters such as Jeremiah the prophet, King David, the harlot Rahab, the pagan widow Ruth, and many others will testify, everyone has a story, yet we do not have to be defined by our stories. Every story is redeemable. Mine was redeemable. Yours is too.

God does just that. He has made provision for that redemption. Our stories, our lives, our understanding can be transformed into purposeful, successful examples of God's grace, mercy, love, and faithfulness. All we need to do is activate it, even if we come from places that the world deems as statistical dregs of society, like I did. Before our births, God has a plan and purpose for our lives. Thankfully, this is what God did for me. He covered me from before birth. I didn't readily recognize this. Once I chose to operate in His system, His way of doing things, I began to see the ways He'd kept me and was with me all along the way, even before I was born.

So, how do we activate God's provision, plan, and purpose? After we choose to operate in His system, God instructs us as to how to change from the system that opposes Him to His way of doing things. Be transformed.

> "...be ye transformed by the renewing of your mind."
> (Romans 12:2 KJV)

We have a choice to conform to what the world, statistics, or anyone else says of us, *or* we can allow the power of God to transform us: to transform our thinking, to transform our way of seeing, to transform our believing. Renewal is key. God did not say of me what the world said, just the opposite. God did not say of me what the statistics said, just the opposite. God gave me a choice to believe what He said or to accept the statistics and thus the fate of those around me. Only by His grace did I accept the choice of His system and way of doing and being. No doubt, had I not made that choice, the statistical predictions would be my lot in life, or more accurately in death. I encourage you to make that same choice and pray that it is so.

POWER POINTS

God says,

"For I know the thoughts that I think toward you ... thoughts of peace, and not of evil, to give you an expected end." (Jeremiah 29:11 KJV)

"For I know the plans I have for you ... plans to prosper you and not to harm you, plans to give you a hope and a future." (Jeremiah 29:11 NIV)

AFFIRMATION

God has a plan and purpose for my life. He planned my purpose even before I was born. God's thoughts toward me are good, and He wants me to have peace. God has an expected end for me, a specific destination. He gives me hope and a bright future ahead. I choose His way and to believe only what He says about me.

CHAPTER 2

———◦———◦———◦———

DESTINY BY TELL-A-VISION

*"And then God answered: 'Write this. Write what you see....
This vision-message is a witness pointing to what's coming. It
aches for the coming – it can hardly wait! And it doesn't lie.
If it seems slow in coming, wait. It's on its way. It will come
right on time.'"* (Habakkuk 2:2-3 MSG)

My first name happens to be of Latino origin. I, however, am not, leastwise not as far as I or my family knows. As was often the case in my culture (and in various cultures, past and present), a young girl soon to be a mother was influenced by popular culture, and my name was selected accordingly. I am often given cause to pause and smile to myself at the workings of Father God by Holy Spirit.

My mommy selected my name from a popular television show at the time of my birth, knowing nothing of the name's origin – although, looking back, perhaps her spirit knew what her natural mind did not. Truly, Holy Spirit caused that name to resonate with Mommy purposefully and strategically, I would say. After my birth, this became apparent to Mommy, and in later years also to me.

Mommy often recounted to me that as a child, she longed for and even prayed for someone of her own to love and to care for. Through unforeseen circumstances, she got what she'd asked for in her first child, me. Just a young teen, she chose my first name from a television show. Ironically, the device and technology of the day was used to tell-a-vision almost in a subliminal way. Mommy found in her firstborn a comfort and a consolation that she had long yearned for over the span of her short life. And that, prophetically, is the meaning of my first name, Consuelo. While Mommy did not have that knowledge intellectually or logically, I have no doubt that her spirit identified with it. The use of the television to tell-a-vision is not the sole indicator.

Being a stickler for academic accuracies, Mommy was sure to read the show credits and spell the name verbatim. Latin languages and dialects often have feminine and masculine versions of words. Some words have only one version, though, and such is my given name. Mommy knew nothing of this at the time of my birth. God did. He knew just the word and call that needed to be spoken over me and into my life. As the eldest of many siblings, as a servant-leader to many children and to those who serve children, I have spent much time comforting, counseling, and consoling others. I did this before I even knew what my name meant, and I continued all the more so after I gained the knowledge. It continues as I attempt to live out my name's meaning and to be an example.

What vision has been set and foretold about you? It may not have been as drastic or as obvious as to come from a tell-a-vision (or a television). Looking back, in what areas of your life can you see the hand, plan, and purpose of God being divinely carried out?

Will you cultivate it, revel in it, act upon it, or deny it? I encourage you to explore and live out the draw and call to who you truly are and who you are truly created to be. If it is not readily apparent, or if it is clouded by the noise of life, do a bit of digging, praying, asking, seeking, reflecting. Acknowledge that you have purpose and significance that started even before your beginning. As Truth is revealed, use it to fulfill purpose and to spark vision in yourself and others. There is great blessing in knowledge and great assurance in being just who you were designed to be!

POWER POINTS

God says,

"I, even I, have spoken; yea, I have called him: I have brought him, and he shall make his way prosperous." (Isaiah 48:15 KJV)

AFFIRMATION

I am unique. I have been created and designed by God specifically to meet a need. I have a name and calling that is selected to be a blessing, an empowerment to prosper, to myself and to others. I purpose to intentionally live out the vision of my call as the blessing God created me to be. As God reveals, I yield. As I yield, I reap a harvest of blessings in return and cause blessings to overflow in the lives of others.

CHAPTER 3

WHERE EVERYBODY KNOWS YOUR NAME

"But now thus saith the Lord that created thee, O Jacob, and He that formed thee, O Israel, Fear not: for I have redeemed thee, I have called thee by thy name; thou art mine." (Isaiah 43:1 KJV)

I have never enjoyed the benefits of popularity or being a part of any exclusive group or clique. So, aside from family, I have never been the known and acknowledged, turn-the-heads-in-the-room sort. I got a taste of this, however, when I would visit my biological father.

While I did not grow up with my biological father, I knew who he was and had visited him at his home on a few occasions in my childhood. Before his early death, my father grew up and lived in the same neighborhood all of my life. As a result, he was very well known there. Not only did everyone know him, but they also knew exactly where he was in the neighborhood at all times. My father's popularity, it would seem, extended to me as well.

Once I came of age, I purposed to spend more time with my father and to build a relationship with him. Unbeknownst to me, that had been established on my father's end all the while I had been growing up.

One of the annual customs of my childhood was school pictures. Each school year from preschool through high school graduation, there was one special day mid-year for school pictures. It was some kind of event in our home. Everyone got new outfits, special hairdos, and money to purchase a package of professional poses, along with a class picture. That is fifteen years of annual photos and several additional special cap-and-gown pose packages for kindergarten, elementary, and high school graduations. I came to find out as an adult that my father owned, displayed, and cherished every single one of the eighteen photographs of me growing up through the years. I found out that not only did he have them on display in his home, but he also took every opportunity to show and share them with everyone he knew over those years.

Whenever I went to see my father once I could do so on my own as an adult, all along the street and in his building people would greet me by name as if they knew me personally. They'd say how good it was to see me. They'd recount how long it might have been since they'd last seen me in person. They'd comment to other neighbors who were in earshot to see who had come to visit. They'd remark how much I still looked like my father. They'd send for my father if they knew he was out and about in the neighborhood. They'd often ask if I remembered them, and I would honestly have to say no, if they waited for a response after my deer-in-the-headlights stare and glazed-over smile.

While it made me quite uncomfortable to arrive into this surreal world where all these people knew me, such that I had some status akin to fame, I realized it was all because of my father. He loved and talked of me so much that all who knew him knew who I was. They knew the years of my life. They welcomed and doted on me when I came to visit, because my father had done so all of my life.

This is a tiny little drop in the bucket when compared to the love of THE Father. Our Heavenly Father cherishes us so much more. He has been with us, orchestrating our lives, desiring a deep, abiding relationship with us all of our days. He has set a special purpose, call, plan, and outcome for our lives (Jeremiah 29:11). Our Father knows you, knows your name, knows all about every year, stage, and event of your life. He brags on us in heaven (Job 1:8, 2:3). He shares information about us with those in the earth and creates divine connections with others for us (Ruth 1:16; 1 Samuel 18:3; John 4:29). He has always waited for us in the same place all the time (Revelation 3:20).

In what ways can you see the handiwork of our Heavenly Father in your life? In what ways has He kept tabs on you and cherished you and bragged on you to others? How has He orchestrated blessings for you when you didn't even realize it? The evidence demonstrates what my earthly father demonstrated: His love. Oh, how our Heavenly Father loves us even the more so (Matthew 7:11). He has demonstrated it to us by giving Himself for us, and further by setting up our life's plan to show how precious we are to Him (Romans 5:8).

POWER POINTS

God says,

"The Lord hath appeared of old unto me, saying, Yea, I have loved thee with an everlasting love: therefore with lovingkindness have I drawn thee." (Jeremiah 31:3 KJV)

"Ye have not chosen me, but I have chosen you, and ordained you, that ye should go and bring forth fruit, and that your fruit should remain..." (John 15:16 KJV)

"See what great love the Father has lavished on us, that we should be called children of God! And that is what we are!" (1 John 3:1a NIV)

AFFIRMATION

God knows me. He knows my name. He loves and cherishes me. He brags on me, His creation, and has made my name known to others. He has purpose and greatness prepared for me. He awaits my love and acceptance in return and has made provision for when I come to Him through Jesus. I am divinely connected to fulfill that designed purpose and to achieve every goal and promise our Heavenly Father has laid out for me.

CHAPTER 4

FAMILY ROOTS

"... I am God, and there is none like me, declaring the end from the beginning, and from ancient times the things that are not yet done, saying, my counsel shall stand, and I will do all my pleasure." (Isaiah 46:9-10 KJV)

"And God said ... and it was so .... And God saw that it was good ..." (Genesis 1 KJV)

God is at the forefront of life even when we fail to recognize it. He has a plan that He orchestrates amidst us, despite us, and because of us. Educators, theorists, and the like once had a buzzword termed "backward design." The idea is that one starts from the desired end result and then builds on the plans and strategies to achieve that result, working from the end backward to the beginning. Now, logic would dictate to start from the beginning with what you know and what you must plan and strategize for the desired outcome. However, backward design can be more effective at identifying the basics of what is needed to achieve a result, and sometimes how to do so in the least possible number of steps.

We are made in the image and likeness of our Father and Creator (Genesis 1:26). I am convinced that the great ideas of any time past, present, and future come directly from our Father's heart, mind, and nature (James 1:17). He knows the end from the beginning. He has orchestrated the events of time, earth, and heaven with the end in mind (Ephesians 1:4; 1 Peter 1:20). The Bible relates this story from beginning to end.

The circumstances of my birth and life were hardly what one would call planned. The world would deem them void of any possible success. God has another designation for seeming impossibilities, though: *"With men this is impossible; but with God all things are possible"* (Matthew 19:26 KJV; see also Mark 10:27 and Luke 18:27). In hindsight, I see that God's hand has been in the mix the whole time, transforming impossibilities of man into His God-possibilities. There were things such as my maternal grandmother having completed a degree in nursing and my resultant healthier lifestyle; my mother and father being very intellectually adept and lovers of knowledge, an affinity that was passed on to me; my mother being introduced to and taking heed to parenting classes that educated young and disadvantaged mothers on how to budget, shop well, and provide healthy and well-balanced meals for their families. All of this and much more evidence of God's handiwork season my life even from before conception like salt and pepper, giving it flavor and essence of its "expected end" planned out by Father God from before the beginning (Jeremiah 29:11).

God has used all the best parts of my life and heritage to overcome many of the negative aspects of my life circumstances. A nursing background developed a focus on, attention to, and maintenance of health and wellness. Healthier choices overcame unhealthy appetites that often drive the poor into adverse physical conditions. A love of learning sparked high academic achievement, opening doors of opportunity. The list goes on. God has blessed me in myriad ways. I am not blessed simply for myself, I am blessed to be a blessing, to be used by God to bless others. God is so confident in this plan of His that He established my end from the beginning. God has set up the best parts of me specifically to cancel out any deviations potentially brought about by adverse circumstances or impossibilities.

What are the best parts of your life and heritage that have the power to combat the worst of circumstances and situations? What are the positive roots Father God has placed within you that make impossibilities possible? For whom are you blessed to be a blessing? What essence, savors, and flavors can you say are evidence of the seasoning of God upon your life (2 Corinthians 2:15; Philippians 4:18)? Allow God to use the best to cancel out the worst.

POWER POINTS

God says,

"Every good thing given and every perfect gift is from above; it comes down from the Father of lights [the Creator and Sustainer of the heavens], in whom there is no variation [no rising or setting] or shadow cast by His turning [for He is perfect and never changes]." (James 1:17 AMP)

"Blessed be the God and Father of our Lord Jesus Christ, who hath blessed us with all spiritual blessings in heavenly places in Christ: according as he hath chosen us in him before the foundations of the world, that we should be holy and without blame before him in love." (Ephesians 1:3-4 KJV)

AFFIRMATION

God knows and sees my end from the beginning. He is the giver of every good, perfect, and perfected gift in me. He has gifted me and empowered me to minister to the needs of others in service to Him. I do so because I love Him and want to be a blessing. God does not change His mind about me. He has established a plan and purpose for me. When I yield to God's plan and purpose, He allows me to see who I really am and to be who He has made me to be. I thank God for my natural family heritage and for the family heritage I have as a part of His family and in relationship with Him.

CHAPTER 5

GRACED

"But by the [remarkable] grace of God I am what I am, and His grace toward me was not without effect. In fact, I worked harder than all of the apostles, though it was not I, but God [His unmerited favor and blessing which was] with me." (1 Corinthians 15:10 AMP)

"If we fought for our rights, we'd be in hell tonight." -Lecrae, "Boasting" (*Rehab*, 2010)

"There, but for the grace of God, goes John Bradford." -John Bradford (quoted in *A Treatise on Prayer* by Edward Bickersteth, 1822)

Illegitimacy was not an uncommon factor in my cultural upbringing. It became more and more common as the decades passed. That is sad to say, but a fact nevertheless. While societal changes and waning cultural structures were no doubt ultimately to blame, this did not negate the individual choices that were made leading to my birth. Others with similar starts in life have quite different stories than mine. But for the grace of God, there go I.

The story of that latchkey kid whose father was incarcerated; whose mom had to leave the home to complete schooling, then join the work force to provide for a large and suddenly single-parent household; whose older brothers were involved in nefarious shenanigans; and whose older sisters were all teen mothers, could have had a much worse ending. Were it not for the grace of God keeping and covering that kid, and her kids, and their kids, the ending would be even sadder than the beginning, no doubt.

Now, some would look at such a lot in life and think, "Why would God allow such horrible circumstances to occur in the lives of these people?" My answer would be, "Grace." And, yes, I would probably get the same look that you are presenting now at such a statement. Although, let us take a different perspective. A young lady who was left unguided or perhaps went against her father's wishes made a choice to be with a young man, tall dark and handsome but with few scruples, and ended up in some shady situations as a result. God watched over her and over the resultant large number of children the couple sired amidst the shady dealings. God protected the house so that the illegal substances and contraband were never found there, and, more importantly, were never found by the children.

God provided that same mama and her brood with education and employment when the young man's dealings caught up with him and he had to spend his sentence away from the family. God kept and protected the children, and their children, in the same way when similar poor choices were made as they grew. God provided a church community for that mama. This church community supported and anchored the family for the rest of that mama's natural life. God enabled that mama and her husband, once released, to purchase a home and raise their remaining children and many grandchildren as well. The children and grandchildren grew into making similar poor decisions along the way, but were always able to come to that mama's home and regroup, resettle, refocus, and reboot. God allowed and used that mama to become the matriarch to four generations of children, grandchildren, great-grandchildren, sisters, brothers, nieces, nephews, neighbors, friends, and fellow parishioners. Was many a poor choice made? Yes! Was many a poor consequence deserved? Absolutely! Were many if not most of the good moments and successes fully undeserved? Totally. What made it turn out for the good, into a legacy of life and love? Grace! God's unmerited favor changed the potential ending. I am a result of that same grace. My life, my accomplishments, my story are a result of that same grace.

While this scenario is not verbatim and not solely unique, it conveys the abbreviated story of my maternal grandmother. That same grace followed my mommy and allowed her to raise her own brood almost twice the size of my grandmother's and spanning a total of three decades. It is *only* by God's grace that not one of her children is incarcerated, not one was violently murdered, not one strung out on illegal substance abuse. This, sadly, has not always been the story of her peers (nor mine, for that matter). Amidst and despite our poor choices and deviations from right and righteous decisions, I can surely see now how God's grace has kept us, has covered us, has protected us.

What circumstances, problems, situations, and results can you look at, or look back to, and see God's handiwork of grace? If you look hard and long enough, I do not doubt that you will be able to see God's grace even in the worst of situations. You, too, will be able to say, "But for the grace of God, there go I." Take some time to think, pray, and ponder on that, selah.

POWER POINTS

God says,

"And he said unto me, My grace is sufficient for thee: for my strength is made perfect in weakness. Most gladly therefore will I rather glory in my infirmities, that the power of Christ may rest upon me." (2 Corinthians 12:9 KJV)

AFFIRMATION

God knows me and every one of my needs. God has graced me. He loves me and grants me undeserved favor because of His great love. God empowers me and grants me favor with others. Even when it doesn't look like it, even when it doesn't feel like it, even when I don't deserve it, God's grace is enough to make all things turn out to be in my favor. I allow God's strength to be perfected when I let His strength shine through and do not attempt to tackle the challenges of life in my own strength, but humbly, through Jesus. I allow God to work in me and through me by the power of Jesus Christ, and I exchange my ignorance for His knowledge, my inabilities for His abilities, my insecurities for His blessed assurance and stability.

CHAPTER 6

NO NORMAL

"So God created man in his own image, in the image of God created he him; male and female created he them." (Genesis 1:27 KJV)

"When I see and consider Your heavens, the work of Your fingers, The moon and the stars, which you have established, What is man that You are mindful of him, And the son of [earthborn] man that You care for him? Yet You have made him a little lower than God, And You have crowned him with glory and honor." (Psalm 8:3-5 AMP)

Far too much of the beginning of my life was spent focusing on being "normal." This was pretty much futile, since by no possible societal standard or expectation could either my birth, my physical appearance, or my life be considered "normal." But the pressure of a culturally induced and media-induced need to "fit in" had me believing the "hype" that there *is* even a such thing as normal. Invariably, of course, I never could fit into what was supposedly deemed as normal. It was not until after many years, and many attempts to fit into places I clearly did not, that I began to recognize that there really is no such thing as "normal." Now, there might be many who disagree with that assessment. However, while normal or norms indicate some standard (and often conformity to a supposed standard), one person's so-called "normal" can be very different from another's because of the simple fact that a standard can always be changed or moved (hence the idea of fads and trends, all quite fleeting, culturally), and because there are always outliers, and because what we call or accept as standard may not be so standard.

The circumstances surrounding my conception, birth, and beginnings in the world were neither ideal nor what was culturally accepted or expected. The mitigating circumstances leading to those humble, albeit atypical, beginnings were fuel for intrusiveness. Many encounters with those outside of my family circle evoked questions and comments that were uncomfortable, awkward, and sometimes simply rude and offensive. When I was an infant and a toddler, my mother bore the brunt of the offenses. Once I became more literate, we shared them.

My facial features were slightly marred at birth. This irregularity was glaringly apparent when I was a child (not so much as an adult, but still apparent). This evoked many a question from adults, children, peers, classmates, neighbors, medical professionals, and the like. Even strangers were emboldened to stare, whisper, and smirk unabashedly and to offer their inquiries. Some queries were delivered in a gentle, covert manner, some downright offensively, some in a bullying and exclusionary way. Regardless of the delivery, it was always quite apparent that there was a difference, giving me no chance of fitting in with what was expected and accepted.

There were also congenital internal abnormalities that impacted the workings of my facial muscles. Whenever I spoke, ate, sang, or engaged in any oral exercise, my facial activity was noticeably different from all others around me. This evoked a whole other set of questions and intrusiveness that only compounded the negative experiences I was subjected to outside of my family circle (and, truth be told, inside that same circle on occasion).

These nuances of my life were combined factors in my inability to ever fit into any category that could be described as normal. These factors did not stop me from learning, playing, thinking, growing, loving, living, but they did keep me from ever being considered normal by others, and they kept me from seeing myself as normal as well. I thought that to be a bad thing for quite some time, probably over a third of my life at this point. But then I learned how much effort, forethought, and creative genius THE Master Designer put into all of creation, all of humanity, all of *me*!

God is a God of variety, v-a-r-i-e-t-y. Just look at all of creation: colors and shapes and sizes, oh my; phyla and genus and species, oh my; waves and coils and curls, oh my; nations and tribes and tongues, oh my; and the lists go on and on, oh my indeed! How is *that* for a twist? THE Master Designer, a Creative Genius, has purposefully made unique differences in all of His handiwork so that no two are exactly the same, even though they are similar and have the same basic make-up. Even those that may seem identical have some particular nuance that characterizes each individual creation alone. Variants can be witnessed everywhere. The very definition of "variant" is that which is not standard. While variants abound and can be seen everywhere and in everything, they all come from One. We have been created in God's image and His likeness. For all our variations, we all have the same basic needs, the same types of desires, the same origin. This commonality is what connects us all and ultimately connects us back to the Master Designer and all of His Creative Genius.

Attempts to make the variations all conform is an egregious offense against the Master Designer and His original plan to see us as the unique individuals He has created us to be in the divine mosaic of humanity. Am I to presume that I, the creation, know better than THE Creator, Lord of all creation? I need not look for, focus on, or attempt to fit into anyone's nonexistent normality box. I have the opportunity to take the view of our Master Designer, our Loving Heavenly Father, and to trust the Creative Genius. I may choose to recognize the variety for what it truly is: a beautifully desirable piece to the divine mosaic. Regardless of the questions, the stares, the rudeness, and the crudeness of others; regardless of humble beginnings, cultural trends, or social expectations and pressures; I can take comfort and joy in the Truth: God makes everyone uniquely in His image and likeness (Genesis 1:27, Psalm 139:14). Thus, "normal" – should there be such a thing, real or imagined – matters not. All that God creates and gives is good, is wonderful, is valuable (Psalm 127:3, James 1:17). That is what matters.

Will you believe and conform to what the world perpetrates, trying to fit in with the cliques, culture, and communities inside their normality box? I challenge you instead to take joy in the divinely orchestrated uniqueness that is the Master Designer's beautifully designed mosaic of humanity. I challenge you to appreciate the variety while connecting with the unifying foundation of the One. Will you rise to the challenge and see yourself as God sees you? Will you give up the effort to conform, and instead enjoy the variety and uniqueness divinely given to you and others while identifying with the commonality that connects us all? May you find a new liberty in that appreciation today and always.

POWER POINTS

God says,

"Ye are blessed of the Lord which made heaven and earth." (Psalm 115:15 KJV)

"I will praise thee; for I am fearfully and wonderfully made: marvellous are thy works; and that my soul knoweth right well." (Psalm 139:14 KJV)

AFFIRMATION

I am a creation of Almighty God, the Lord of all creation. All that He makes and has made is good. I am wonderfully made and uniquely created by God to be the exact individual to which He has purposed my specific and unique design. There is none other exactly like me. God has made me one of a kind, priceless, and invaluable. He has designed, sees, and knows my use and worth. He has divinely created me just as I am and like no other. My Heavenly Father takes joy and finds pleasure in my every nuance, which He has created and specifically designed. There never has been and never will be another exactly like me.

CHAPTER 7

---◆---◉---◆---

WHAT'S IN A NAME

"... For I know you well and you are special to me. I know you by name." (Exodus 33:17 MSG)

In many cultures past and present, names are chosen and given with great purpose and ceremony. Names in these cases are recognized as having meaning and power to thrust the recipient into specific destiny (destination); names represent a call. In some Latin-based languages, the actual word used for "name" means "called." Shakespeare wrote in his epic stage play *Romeo and Juliet*, "What's in a name? That which we call a rose by any other name would smell as sweet." Perhaps not. While this has a beautiful poetic ring to it, I submit that names are words, and words have power (Proverbs 18:21, Mark 11:23). Words are like seeds; given the nurture of continued use, and given the soil of our ear-gates and our minds, they produce (Isaiah 55:11, John 6:63). And seeds always produce after their own kind, whether need seeds or weed seeds (Genesis 1:12, 8:22).

Many biblical characters had their names changed by God Himself. They were called to a specific purpose and destination and given a new name to complement the corresponding call. Some were given their names by God prenatally or at birth. Every time these characters were spoken to or spoken about, their destinies (destinations) were called out and spoken as seeds ready to produce. It would seem that our loving and faithful Heavenly Father has no problem identifying who we are in the earth and ensuring that is what is called into existence. This is true for biblical characters, and by God's divine providence, this is also my story.

My mommy, being quite young at the time of my birth and having gone through the trauma of birth and delivery as all new mothers do, was impacted dramatically by the processes of being with child, birth, and delivery. She imagined that there was no way she would go through the experience of having more children (nothing further from the truth there, for she went on to birth children for another three decades, literally). Mommy, hence, thought to give me all of the names she imagined she would have given the children she was never going to have. Counting my surname, I have a total of five names. That alone is an anomaly in my ethnic culture and in the culture of my nation. Usually, a person is given three names at most: a first name, middle name, and a last name. When asked my middle name, I would reply that I didn't have one. Technically, I did not have one; I had three.

I mention divine providence because of the nature of my names. Mommy, being a young just-barely-teen, did not have the forethought to actually look up name meanings and the like. Her choices were the result of popular culture and fleeting friendships of the time. However, God's handiwork is quite evident when you investigate the meanings and the combinations of the words used to designate how I was called (remember, "name" can mean "call" or "called"). My first name means "consolation." My second name can mean "of my mother," or "delicate." My third name means "grace." My fourth name means "noble." My surname means "ingenuity," "wit," or "clever." On many occasions when I was growing up, Mommy would belt out all five names in a bit of a frustrated tizzy to get my attention. In learning to write my name as a preschooler and kindergartener, I first learned the first name. Once I learned all my letters, I often practiced writing the entire listing of the five (ironically, by this time, I had three little sisters; turns out there were still names available in the repertoire).

Words have power. Words are like seeds. Words produce. Every time the list was belted out, every time I wrote it, every time I spoke and rehearsed the list, it was sent out to produce. Every single time the seed was spoken, it was spoken to produce: the consolation of my mother, delicate, gracious, noble, with clever wit and ingenuity. Every single time the seed was written, it was written to produce: the consolation of my mother, delicate, gracious, noble, with clever wit and ingenuity. Who could have known that the seed of that list of five names would become my call? It was, after all, what I was called. It is what I still am today, and what the seed of that word power, that call, has produced. I, Consuelo Delilah Nannette Patrice Gaines, am the consolation of my mother, delicate, gracious, noble, with clever wit and ingenuity. Really, just ask my siblings, my parents, my close friends and family, my coworkers, my neighbors. Not boasting on me at all, but on the orchestration and implementation of God at work on my behalf for what He needed, because, by the grace of God, I am what I am (1 Corinthians 15:10).

What's in a name? What is your name? What are you called? What word power is daily being spoken, written, planted of you? To what destination (destiny) will it bring you? Even a nickname is a word and has power if that is what you are called, what is spoken over you, what is being nurtured by continued use and what produces given the soil of your ear-gates and your mind. Is it incidental, accidental, or providential? Remember, when necessary, God changed a person's name to align with their call, with what needed to be produced. Research it. Study it out. Pray on it. Then observe the many ways, past and present, that it is producing. Then live it out purposefully for God.

POWER POINTS

God says,

"Thou shalt no more be termed Forsaken; neither shall thy land any more be termed Desolate: but thou shall be called Hephzibah, and thy land Beulah: for the Lord delighteth in thee, and thy land shall be married." (Isaiah 62:4 KJV)

AFFIRMATION

God calls me by the name that He has established over me. My God-given name has power to produce. I am just who God says I am and needs me to be to fulfill the call He has on my life and to reach the destination (destiny) that He has set for me from the beginning. As I speak forth my name and as others speak my name, my name produces exactly who and what God needs me to be.

In The Beginning

In The Beginning

This next section reflects on the beginnings in my life, the time period of the wonderment, innocence, and resilience of a young child. Without the hindrances and limitations of biases and restrictive societal influences, young children have an uncanny way of breaking things down to simply the basic needs. The 17th-century theorist John Locke used the term "blank slate." I rather think of it as the absence of drama and the pursuit of abiding connection. It is easy for me to see why Jesus Himself said you must come as a little child in order to connect with Kingdom principles (Luke 18:16-17).

CHAPTER 8

I WAS BORN FOR THIS

"According as he hath chosen us in him before the foundation of the world, that we should be holy and without blame before him in love..." (Ephesians 1:4 KJV)

Contrary to popular belief, everyone is born with innate inclinations and tendencies. There is that something on the inside that parents and close family can see evidence of from birth (probably even from conception). Sadly, not everyone homes in on these propensities. Some discount them, some ignore them, some lose sight of them, some repeatedly bounce between knowing and not. I, unlike many in my culture, always seemed to identify with my innate inclinations and tendencies, even as a young child. I never struggled with what to be when I grew up or what to do with my life. I cannot rightly say why. If left to guess, I would say I was pretty headstrong about what moved me. I have a fierce tendency toward loyalty, sometimes to a fault. So, once an idea, a thought, a person, a concept moves me, I don't give it up or release it easily.

This can be both rewarding on one hand, and extremely dangerous on the other. Thus, I have learned to take life, ideas, thoughts, concepts, and people with great caution, especially that which moves me. I have also learned to accept that this is a part of my make-up. It is a gift. As with all gifts, it has great potential for aiding me well in life; yet, as with all gifts, misuse or abuse has great potential for detriment. As in the famous cases of the zealous disciple Simon Peter (Matthew 16:33, 26:75) and the greatly learned religious leader Saul of Tarsus (Acts 8-9), excessive fervor in fierce loyalty can backfire without the tempering of Truth and agape Love (Isaiah 29:13; Matthew 15:8).

I entered the world of formal education just shy of my third birthday. I have had a love affair with it and with our houses of learning called schools ever since. When I saw the person at the front of the class moving about and sharing knowledge so kindly and lovingly, I was hooked. Something clicked, or snapped, or locked, or tripped. From that moment to this, it was ALL I wanted to do, to be, to identify with. I couldn't, wouldn't, and refused to shake it. It would not let me go, and I didn't want it to. I "practiced" and mimicked that same inclination on my siblings, my friends, my neighbors. I studied and catered to my teachers to observe and learn their craft. As a youth, I tutored kids and even adults at every opportunity. One of my first summer volunteer services was teaching local immigrants the basics of English.

This is my earliest memory of such an innate inclination and tendency. Looking back over my life, I can see God's hand in the gifting of other such propensities as well. He made me the eldest of many siblings, establishing the gift and qualities of leadership and diplomacy. He gifted me with excellent literacy skills, which have opened a world of writing, public speaking, and building curriculum. He gifted me with many siblings and blended families, sharpening a love for children and people that carries over professionally and socially. That same gift of a large family has also taught me patience and compassion.

I once was one who discounted the benefits of the giftings and the innate inclinations that were mine from the start. After recognizing them, life became more meaningful, more enjoyable, more purposeful. I began to realize and to recognize that God gave me my various giftings not only as a joy to myself, but also as a help to others. He also began to give me a respect for the variety of innate inclinations and tendencies that we all have. God forbid that someone force me to clock in as a technology company CEO or a professional barrister or a mechanical engineer. We need people with those innate inclinations and tendencies as well. Lord knows I have needed to hire some of them, and I have friends who fall into those categories with just as much fervor and zeal as I do in my own innate tendencies.

I can stand firm in my giftings and have a heart of gratitude for them, and I can allow others to do the same in theirs. I recognize that I was born for this, for exactly what I am doing and thriving in right now. I also recognize that each person I encounter is in the same position. They were born for their innate inclinations, tendencies, and abilities. God has set us up in all the ways necessary for us to contribute to the world individually and corporately. When we recognize and settle on what we were created for, we thrive, and we cause others to thrive. When we are grateful for who we are and what we have, we can be grateful for others in the same way. There is a certain glorious satisfaction in contentedness. I can still learn, grow, and allow others to do the same, from a place of gratitude and a desire to share with and contribute to the world around me. I find that most fulfilling.

What are you born for? Have you taken the opportunity to recognize your innate inclinations and tendencies? Have you valued the gifting within you? What has God gifted to you to flow and operate in? Will you purpose to value your giftings AND the giftings of others? Will you find fulfillment in that contentedness? I invite you to do so. I invite you into the glorious satisfaction of contentedness. If you happen to be one who has discounted, ignored, or lost sight of your innate God-given gifts that drive your inclinations and tendencies, it is never too late to pray, reflect, and rediscover what you were expressly created for, designed for, and assigned to for the purpose of contributing to the world around you and for fulfillment. We were born for this!

POWER POINTS

God says,

"God's various expressions of power are in action everywhere; but God himself is behind it all. Each person is given something to do that shows who God is: Everyone gets in on it, everyone benefits.... The variety is wonderful..." (1 Corinthians 12:6-7 MSG)

"...to each one is given the manifestation of the Spirit [the spiritual illumination and the enabling of the Holy Spirit] for the common good." (1 Corinthians 12:7 AMP)

AFFIRMATION

God has created me with innate inclinations, tendencies, and gifts, which are designed for me to take joy in them and for them to bring contentedness to my life. I am just who God says I am, and I am just who God needs me to be in order to operate in an attitude of gratitude and to contribute to the world around me. God has established this from my beginning and for my benefit. I value the gifts imparted to me and the gifts of others. I seek out, find, and thrive in the application of every innate, God-given ability within me, and God's gifts propel me toward my destiny (my destination) for a fruitful and productive life.

CHAPTER 9

THE GOOD LIFE

"Verily I say unto you, whosoever shall not receive the kingdom of God as a little child shall in no wise enter therein." (Luke 18:17 KJV)

"I assure you and most solemnly say to you, whoever does not receive the kingdom of God [with faith and humility] like a child will not enter it at all." (Luke 18:17 AMP)

Growing up, I don't think I ever really realized that we were what society might call poor. It probably was not until late high school or early college that I even began to identify with that thought or idea. I have, for the most part, been rather slow on the uptake socially. I have never truly caught on to the latest fads, fashions, or colloquialisms.

My life probably could be categorized as rather sheltered, all things considered. And, although my family was large, nomadic, transitory, and received public assistance for the better part of my childhood, I probably lived more of a "Pollyanna" life than most who were of a similar background. It could perhaps have to do with the fact that I ate three square meals a day, plus a couple of snacks and dessert, and that I was always a well-clothed and well-groomed child. A child's needs aren't usually all that complicated. Simplicity is the order of the day for most children. As a child, this rang true for me.

I wasn't very popular. In fact, I could probably be categorized as more of a nerd, even from early childhood. Not having name brands or the latest fashions or what some might deem as stylish attire was never really a big factor for me. This was true from the very beginnings and throughout my childhood, probably into early adulthood.

As a child, I ate well. I was clothed well. I had a pretty stable roof over my head most times. I never identified with being poor, even though the annual income of my single parent (who, off and on, was not always single), would categorize us as poor, and even very poor, probably just shy of living in run-down infested domiciles (okay, rarely in run-down infested domiciles, though not early on), or just shy of being put out in the street or having utilities cut off, and the like. Thankfully, God has been gracious to me and my family. Prior to becoming aware of the fact that, according to society's categories, my family was considered very poor, I felt like I lived a wonderful life; I still feel that way looking back. I felt loved every single day and was properly cared for every single day. I felt like I was clean. I looked decent for the most part, and my family did as well. So, for a very long time, I was clueless to what others may have known to be facts: that according to society, we were at the bottom, and that there probably wasn't even hope for us to get to the top after Mommy's second husband, fifth child, and second divorce – leastwise, not according to societal statistics and projections. We may have been considered more of a living, true-to-life urban ghetto saga whose characters were headed for the bottom of the barrel.

At the very same time of this societal plight in which I was one of the primary characters, I walked around and lived life in joy and happiness, having many opportunities and doors opened to me, never knowing what I might have been missing. *That* is the good life: the place of contentment, where all your basic needs are met and you do not really want for anything, not truly. There is nothing you really need. Everything you truly need is there: love, companionship, family, food, clean water, clothing that fits, a new hairdo every day. There is absolutely nothing you need. I was not privy to how all I had was provided or to the sacrifices that were made to ensure that I had all that I needed. That is the good life.

That is the life that I found out God wants us to live and have right here in the now. Many times, I had heard it taught in various religious denominations that it will all be better in the "sweet by and by." It will all work out in the "sweet by and by" when we get to heaven. That is when everything will be wonderful and joyous. I will feel that all my needs are met. However, when I look back on my life as a kid and how joyous it was – how oblivious I was to what society may have deemed "less than" in my life – I am given cause for pause. I was oblivious to what society may have projected that I lacked and said I should have been discontented with. I was able to enjoy life, to enjoy my mommy, to enjoy my sisters and eventually brothers too, to enjoy chores and school and celebration days, never knowing what the world thought I might've been missing, the good life. Oh, for those days of innocence and wonder, contentedness, contentment, and joy.

Now, that is not to say that life didn't have its ups and downs or its challenges, or that I didn't see commercials and want the latest toy. It's to say that my needs were met, I was satisfied with that, and being absolutely satisfied with that is quite like no other feeling. I was oblivious to the fact that others were looking at my circumstances and thinking how bad they must be. For me, it wasn't bad at all. I was living the good life. I *am* living the good life. When I came to faith, I had to relearn that attitude. I had to recognize that God *had* provided *everything* that I needed. It doesn't matter what the newest fad is, or what society says I should or shouldn't have or buy, or where I should or shouldn't live, or what occupation I should or shouldn't pursue. What society says doesn't really matter.

My Father in heaven, Who provides all of the things that I need, Who is my all sufficiency, has established what is necessary for me to have, and He has made every provision for the need. Every one of my needs being already met and provided for puts me in a place of contentment, a place that recognizes Father's love for me and that extends a heart of gratitude for all of the provision He has ALREADY made and has promised to make continually. The good life.

What has society tried to make us dissatisfied with, in which our Heavenly Father wants us to find contentment? What has society deemed as "less than," that our Heavenly Father says is sufficient? In what areas might we need to stop, step back, reevaluate, and say, "You know what? I may want this, that, or the other. It may seem good; but, God *is* good. I really do have everything that I *need*." Anything that I may need and don't have, when I ask and make the request, Father God is faithful to provide it, right when I need it. He never fails and never will. The things that I may desire and want, He surprises me with on occasion, or He makes provision for them before I even ask. Sometimes I just think a thought, and then, lo and behold, Faithful, Loving, Gracious Father that He is, He gets it to me. He does so because He loves me. The good life.

May we all find that place of recognizing how good God is to us, of recognizing that He has made every provision for us and that we can come with a heart of gratitude for that provision, take joy in it, and be content, no matter what the world says, no matter what society's expectations may be, no matter what "the Joneses" have or don't have. I challenge us today to recognize and to live the good life.

POWER POINTS

God says,

"... godliness with contentment is great gain." (1 Timothy 6:6 KJV)

"Therefore do not worry or be anxious (perpetually uneasy, distracted) ... for your heavenly Father knows that you need ... But first and most importantly seek (aim at, strive after) ... [His way of doing and being right – the character of God], and all these things will be given to you also." (Matthew 6:31-33 AMP)

"But my God shall supply all your need according to his riches in glory by Christ Jesus." (Philippians 4:19 KJV)

AFFIRMATION

God knows my every need. God knows and makes provision for my every need. God knows, makes provision for, and supplies my every need. God has no lack and no shortage. He is my good Heavenly Father, and He has and gives to me more than enough to thrive and to live the good life He has planned and purposed just for me. I rest assured, contented, and secure in God's abundant provision for me. Should there be anything I need or desire, I will go to God and trust Him as my Source for every resource. I will not worry or fear or engage in dissatisfaction with my circumstance or situations. I will count every blessing and gift from God and maintain an attitude of gratitude for every blessing and every provision in my life.

CHAPTER 10

I HAD A PRAYING GRANDMOTHER

"Teach them to your children. Talk about them when you are at home and when you are away, when you are resting and when you are working." (Deuteronomy 11:19 GNB)

"Teach them well to your children, talking about them when you sit at home and walk along the road, when you lie down and when you get up." (Deuteronomy 11:19 NCV)

As a young child, once I became skilled enough to find my way from point A to point B in our neighborhood, my mommy would send me off on Sundays to my maternal grandmother's church, which was in our neighborhood. My grandmother was a former resident of the neighborhood but no longer lived there, as she had experienced a recent transition into the joys of home ownership. Mommy, who, at the time, had me, two toddlers, and an infant at home, as well as an incarcerated husband, found it rather harrying to get everyone together and out of the house at the same time, so she did so only out of necessity or for specific purposes. I was also an early riser, so that may have contributed to Mommy being glad to send me off to church with my grandmother.

My grandmother's church welcomed me and our entire family, always, with open arms. I would often arrive before my grandmother, since she occasionally worked on Sundays. She lived on another side of town and didn't drive, so she had to travel a lengthy commute to get to church. I would often be there when the doors opened, but there were times when Granny was not. The congregation took me in, sat me in Sunday School, nurtured me, and showed me how to find passages in the Bible.

My grandmother was a bit of a legend at her church. During Sunday service, there was a specific time when everyone would rise and stand and be able to speak public prayers. There was no specific order. As you found it in your heart to speak up and speak out, you could go forth in prayer, and anyone in the congregation could take turns to do so. My grandmother was well known, for the entire tenure of her membership in her church, for rendering prayers that pushed the patience of the younger attendees. Granny would go forth and pour her heart out to God, at each opportunity, in long soliloquy supplications no shorter than about three to five minutes. Five minutes of oral prayer (sometimes longer) was taxing to some of the younger membership. Even those in our family, like my cousins, would often groan audibly as Granny would begin her prayers, because they knew they were in for quite a wait before the next person could pray, and before they could return to their seats, and before service could be that much closer to being over.

I was always fascinated at the length of Granny's prayers; fascinated at how *much* she had to say to God; fascinated at how she could, on the spur of the moment, think of *so many* things to say, for *so* long. I would often think and wonder: what was the record? How long could she really go? To a young child, the endurance and focus that it took to offer everything that is attached to your life might seem like it should be short and easy. It should probably have taken less than a minute, not five to ten times longer.

As I grew as a child, my mother began to take on that same role. She would have long, extensive prayers. Over time, I began to realize that these long, extensive prayers were because there was so much to pray for.

As I came into adulthood, my own prayers began to be extended as well. I wanted to call out in the conversation with my Heavenly Father all of the people, places, and things upon my heart. Even though I began to realize and recognize that Father already knew them, there is power in words, in intercession, in standing in the gap. Others around me, ones I didn't even recognize as people of faith, would come and ask me to pray, would send messages and ask if I would pray for their family, for themselves, for their health, for a tragedy or sickness. My prayers began to get longer and longer, and the list began to grow and grow. Suddenly there didn't seem to be enough time to get all the needs, petitions, observations, inquiries, listening, and requests in. I would often think back to those stints of time when my grandmother would pray out loud in church, and how it would seem so long to my cousins that they'd groan about it. I would think on how my young mind would wonder at the length of Granny's prayers and the number of things that she would come up with to say. I began to realize there is *so* much to pray for. There are so many who have needs and wants, desires and issues. I inherited the mantle I saw as a young child, though I could not have fathomed it at the time. The heritage that was my grandmother's, and then my mother's, became mine.

Granny took her leave some years ago and went on to heaven before us, as it should be. She left a legacy, and oftentimes I think of her and her reputation for praying long and praying hard and praying strong. I wonder how many times she prayed for me. I wonder how many of the blessings of my life are because others prayed for me with that kind of length and strength and fervor. I am grateful for the length and strength of Granny's prayers. Granny knew things that I had yet to learn when I would hear her pray as a child. I am grateful to God for that heritage. I am grateful for having learned the purpose of the length and strength of prayers: to connect with my Heavenly Father and to pour my heart out, to build relationship with Him as he responds and reacts and engages in the conversation of prayer with me.

What divine relationship connection is a part of your heritage, known or unknown? Will you stop and take a moment to be grateful for that? Will you choose to be grateful for whatever was in your heritage and in your past and in your growth that has led you to build relationship with our Heavenly Father? Will you be grateful for that which has led you to choose the life that God has designed for you? Such an attitude of gratitude and such a heritage can lead you to counting the blessings that you have: past, present, and those to come.

POWER POINTS

God says,

"The heartfelt and persistent prayer of a righteous man (believer) is able to accomplish much [when put into action and made effective by God – it is dynamic and can have tremendous power]." (James 5:16b AMP)

"Lo, children are an heritage of the Lord: and the fruit of the womb is his reward." (Psalm 127:3 KJV)

AFFIRMATION

God has given to me a unique and specific heritage. My background and life experiences prepare me to walk in the destiny that God has designed for me. God's plan for my life is purposeful and good. His purpose is what is best for me and brings out the best in me. I commit to be thankful and pleased with the heritage with which God has graced me. I yield and submit to His plan and purpose that enables and empowers me to bless and help others. I am prepared for this and for every moment to which God brings me.

CHAPTER 11

PROJECTS, AND PRISONS,
AND PINTS, OH MY

"Having predestinated us unto the adoption of children by Jesus Christ to himself, according to the good pleasure of his will..." (Ephesians 1:5 KJV)

"He predestined and lovingly planned for us to be adopted to Himself as [His own] children through Jesus Christ, in accordance with the kind intention and good pleasure of His will..." (Ephesians 1:5 AMP)

"God had already decided that through Jesus Christ he would make us his sons and daughters – this was his pleasure and purpose." (Ephesians 1:5 GNB)

My mommy (who was wedded in holy matrimony thrice) and my father were never united in holy matrimony. I was a product of their union, just not a matrimonial one. My mommy, as a young teen who was determined to be a parent, just without the ideological constraints of our western society and culture, had few options when she found herself in her mid-teens with a toddler and an infant on the way. Thus, Mommy proceeded to enter into her first matrimonial union in her mid-teen years, her groom a mere few months her senior.

The couple, with a now-growing family, took up residence shortly thereafter in what was at that time a haven for many in similar situations and circumstances: urban housing development projects. Monikers such as "concrete jungle" and "projects" were bestowed upon these large, cell-like, multi-dwelling structures that, over the course of a couple of decades, became assortments of the forgotten, the weak, the disenfranchised, the addicted, the poor (in finance and in spirit). In the course of time and opportunity, these dwellings became safe havens for crime, violence, gangs, drugs, hopelessness, helplessness, and cradle-to-the-grave by direct route, "do not pass go, do not collect $200."

Such were the formative years of my life. The aforementioned husband spent many of those years incarcerated. Thus, while documents stated a two-parent household, reality dictated otherwise. My father lived in that assortment all of my life, up until his death. Far more favored than most of the male populace there, my father completed a tenure of five decades and became a staple, if not a pillar, of that community. He took to alcohol, and later other substances, and was never quite able to relinquish the hold. I imagine sobriety is overrated in a "concrete jungle."

Yet, despite the "projects" and prisons and pints, God was there. Amidst the "concrete jungle," God was there. Amidst the poverty, violence, gangs, addiction, hopelessness, and helplessness, God was there. I know this only in hindsight. Amidst that same assortment, God covered me, kept me, preserved me, and brought about good. The humble beginnings of those formative years were not my making; yet God saw fit to make me out of that same assortment. God saw fit to cover Mommy and her babies. He opened doors of opportunity. He cultivated seeds of knowledge, information, growth, and experience that drew me to Him and into my destiny. Thanks be unto God for the grace to accept the draw. Thanks be to God for those who, all along the way, and perhaps before I even saw the light of day (figuratively and literally), were praying for me.

"Projects" and prisons and pints don't have to define us, don't have to limit us, don't have to thwart our destiny (destination). No matter where we are from, no matter our heritage, no matter our environment, no matter what the world says, no matter the lessons along the way, we can grab hold to the destiny (destination) that has been prepared for us, pre-pared for us, pre-destined for us; and it is NEVER too late to do so (nor too early, for that matter). What areas of life is God drawing you from, out of, and in spite of? What pre-destination is calling to you? What other destinations (destinies) are attempting to keep you off course? Perhaps it is something other than projects, prisons, or pints. Whatever may be attempting to kick you off course or keep you there, rest assured, there is NOTHING too hard for God! He is a master at turning trouble into triumphs, problems and pitfalls into personal and professional accomplishments, fierce formative years into fabulous fulfillment (Isaiah 61:3; 2 Corinthians 2:14).

POWER POINTS

God says,

"To appoint unto them that mourn in Zion, to give unto them beauty for ashes, the oil of joy for mourning, the garment of praise for the spirit of heaviness; that they may be called trees of righteousness, the planting of the Lord, that he may be glorified." (Isaiah 61:3 KJV)

"Behold, I am the Lord, the God of all flesh: is there any thing too hard for me?" (Jeremiah 32:27 KJV)

AFFIRMATION

The troubles of my life, my past, and my upbringing do not dictate my today nor my tomorrow. I am not limited by circumstances. I am not limited by my environment or by things I may have lacked. God is all sufficient and has designed me not just to survive, but to thrive. God is all sufficient, and there is nothing too hard for Him. He provides all I need to make it to the proper destination (destiny) and to exchange every negative element for that which is positive, and for that which will usher me into the precise plan and purpose He has for me. I embrace the positive, precise plan and purpose God has pre-destined for me. I yield to the draw and heed the call ... yes, and amen.

CHAPTER 12

UNDENIABLE HERITAGE

"Through our union with Christ we too have been claimed by God as his own inheritance. Before we were even born, he gave us our destiny; that we would fulfill the plan of God who always accomplishes every purpose and plan in his heart."
(Ephesians 1:11 TPT)

When people see me with my mother, they often comment how similar our features are; even our physical build is similar. This commentary has been made for most of my life – that is, until they would see me with my father. There was an undeniable awareness that I was the image of my father, from the facial shape to the proportion of our features. There was no mistaking at any time, if anyone saw my father and me together in person or in a photograph, that there was a definite heritage and relationship.

I didn't grow up with my father, not in the sense that he was in my household. We would visit him every now and again when I was a child. As an adult, I grew much closer to him. I had the opportunity to see him more frequently and to engage with him in conversation, in fellowship, in relationship. When I was a little girl and had occasion to encounter my father, whether a brief visit or in passing, everyone around us would comment on how much I looked like him. And it was true. There was no denying that I was, to use the common colloquialism, the "spitting image" of my father, barring a slight ocular marring of my facial features.

When it comes to behaviors and nuances, tendencies, and ways of thinking, reacting, and engaging with others, I could not tell you whether that same heritage would be undeniable with my father. I can, however, tell you that it is undeniable when it comes to my mother; I could probably go so far back as to say my grandmother as well, and definitely an uncle and aunt or two and some cousins. When comparing notes, we tend to think in the same ways, to act in the same ways, to react the same, to respond the same, to even have similar ideas and professions. In reference to these similarities, Mommy likes to say, in a dramatic sort of way, "Dum da da dummm … she's just like *(dramatic pause)*, just like *(dramatic pause)*, her motherrrrrr… *(in a superhero announcer kind of way)*." Whenever those heritage similarities and nuances pop up – forgetfulness here, a wacky and wayward comment there, a paper stack here, a kooky collection there – Mommy chuckles or outright laughs out loud and comments in her dramatic way with her coined phrase. Yes, the heritage there is undeniable too.

While my father has very distinctly set and categorized my physical features and outward appearance, Mommy has done the same for my way of thinking, responding, reacting, engaging in life with others, and my way of engaging with problems, with circumstances, with situations, and perhaps even with my Heavenly

Father. Heritage is undeniable. Scientists will tell us that our DNA will pinpoint, with all accuracy, exactly who we are, where we've come from, and to whom we are connected.

I'm sure God has that awareness without the DNA markers. I'm sure that He has a hand in forming and formulating exactly who we are and who we become. He has told us in His Word that He wants our spiritual heritage to be undeniably linked to Him (Genesis 1:27; Leviticus 20:7; 1 Peter 1:16; John 15:5). He calls to us (Isaiah 45:4). He draws us (John 12:32). He patiently waits for us, knocking at the door of our hearts (Revelation 3:20), orchestrating life so that our paths continue to encounter Him and encounter His love (1 John 3:1), His grace, and His mercy toward us and for us (Lamentations 3:22-23), so that when we accept the call to become adopted and become His (Galatians 4:4-6), our heritage – our spiritual heritage, the newness of life that He gives us – is undeniable.

Jesus said it best: you'll know them by their fruit (Matthew 7:20). Just as you'll know a tree by its fruit, you'll know your heritage by its fruit, by what is produced. It is undeniable. Visit the produce section of any store or market. What is produced undeniably came from that same item's fruit (where the seed is located). Apple seeds make apple trees, which produce apples. Grape seeds make vines, which produce grapes. Celery seeds produce stalks, which produce celery. Love seeds produce actions that are the fruit and evidence of love. Anger seeds produce actions and words that are the fruit and evidence of anger. Patience seeds produce actions and kindness that are the fruit and evidence of patience. It is the same for all things:

what's inside, the internal makeup, is what is going to come out and show up on the outside.

Who do you look like physically, mentally, emotionally? What heritage shines through? Most importantly, who do you look like spiritually? Is your spiritual heritage undeniable? Do you look like the world and everyone else around you that is projected in the media, or connected to flighty and temporary things that may not matter tomorrow and certainly won't matter in eternity? Or perhaps, do you look like God, our Father, just like Jesus? Do you look like agape love in the realm of your spirit? Do you look like forgiveness and mercy and grace in your spirit and in the way that you interact with others around you? Heritage is undeniable. God awaits us to come to Him, to identify with Him in His heritage of faith and love. Will you deny your true heritage or embrace it?

POWER POINTS

God says,

"Giving thanks unto the Father, which hath made us meet to be partakers of the inheritance of the saints in light..." (Colossians 1:12 KJV)

"...always thanking the Father. He has enabled you to share in the inheritance that belongs to his people, who live in the light." (Colossians 1:12 NLT)

"Ye shall know them by their fruits.... Even so every good tree bringeth forth good fruit; but a corrupt tree bringeth forth evil fruit. A good tree cannot bring forth evil fruit, neither can a corrupt tree bring forth good fruit.... Wherefore by their fruits ye shall know them." (Matthew 7:16a, 17-18, 20 KJV)

"This is the heritage of the servants of the Lord, and their righteousness is of me, saith the Lord." (Isaiah 54:17b KJV)

"'This is what God's servants can expect. I'll see to it that everything works out for the best.' God's Decree." (Isaiah 54:17b MSG)

AFFIRMATION

I am made up of all that God needs in me to carry out His plan and purpose for my life. I have a heritage that is established by God, even the unseemly parts. God is well able to take all the parts of me to bring forth what is good, what is needed, what fulfills

His call on my life, what fulfills my life's purpose. There is nothing too hard for God. God works all things for the good of those who love Him. I love God, therefore I have divine favor that causes all things to work for my good. I go forth in boldness and confidence, knowing that I have a heritage that has set me up for success and for my destiny.

CHAPTER 13

DISCOVER TO UNCOVER

"Those whom God had already chosen he also set apart to become like his Son, so that the Son would be the eldest brother in a large family." (Romans 8:29 GNB)

I don't remember a whole lot of my life as a young child. However, there are specific vivid memories that I have from that time, and there are also incidents I can remember from when I was a young child that colored the rest of my life. I didn't find out until later in life, almost adulthood, that this was not common for most people.

One of my most vivid memories is starting school. When I was a little girl, there were centers in specific communities to reach what we now may call "at-risk" children and families, communities and populations that may have needed more of a start in life, at least as perceived by the government and funding sources. One such child-parent center was in my neighborhood as a young child. It served early and mid-level preschoolers and kindergartners and their families. At the end of your time in the early childhood center, you'd graduate from kindergarten and go to the "big" school, the elementary school.

These educational centers also had special services for parents. There was a specific room for parents to gain knowledge about nutrition, child-rearing, budgeting, finances, and more, through classes, provided resources, and workshops. The idea was to assist the families in giving their children a better start in life through education, resources, and support.

I started attending our neighborhood child-parent center at almost three years old and was enamored from that moment on. I was enthralled not only with the school environment and the set of peers and activities that we got to participate in, but also with the people I got to see every day, who poured into my life and the lives of my peers. While attending the center, I spent joyous times singing songs, eating yummy healthy foods, engaging with peers, and having warm, kind, encouraging words spoken to and over me all the time. There were also rest times and nap times where we got a chance to relax and reenergize. During that lie down and rest time, there was also soft music playing and/or calming soothing voices, dim lights, just a pleasurable experience. Not to mention that I happened to be very astute at academia, so the staff that worked with us, teachers, assistants, and volunteers always had wonderful words and encouragement for me. I was forever impressed, and the impression was deep and abiding. I recognize now that not everyone has had such excellent experiences in school.

Truth be told, not every single one of my school years could be categorized as excellent, nor every single one of my instructors. But when one is so impressively enamored with something, at least for me, there's no deterrent that can detract from the joy. I only see joy in it, "rose-colored glasses" and all. What I discovered in that nurturing, encouraging, joyful environment was that it was the kind of environment I wanted forever and always in my little child mind. That's how I would describe it. Grownups today might describe it as life purpose, or a life calling, or another such adult term. For me, I never wanted to leave that joy, and it only got better and better.

Thus, I discovered what I wanted to connect myself with for the rest of my life. It never changed from that moment on. I wanted the joy to continue. I wanted to keep that warm, fuzzy feeling of contentment and satisfaction that seemed to be better than almost any other thing. I wanted to teach. I wanted to be that person who was there up in the front, sharing knowledge, nurturing, giving, and exciting others. I wanted to stay in that house of knowledge and any building of joy like it, with the singing, learning, and knowledge abounding. I almost couldn't get enough of it.

Once that discovery was made, it empowered me to uncover resolve, diligence, perseverance, and commitment. That discovery empowered me to uncover a resolve to seek out whatever I could to make teaching and learning my end. Some would call that a goal or a dream or a mission. That discovery empowered me to be diligent in learning as much as I could so that I could share as much as I learned. That discovery empowered me to persevere through the hard moments and incidents of life and learning, with the focus in mind to fulfill that resolve and to continue to do so diligently. That discovery empowered me to commit to taking that resolve and diligence as far as it would go, for as long as it would go, and to make it do so for as long as possible. As a young child, I had no concept of any of those ideas or definitions. I could not have verbalized or explained the discovery at that time, but it is what drove me. I couldn't have explained what it led me to uncover. I just knew I had to seek after teaching and follow that draw, to pursue it, and that no matter what, it would be worth it.

That feeling and resolve to maintain and perpetuate that initial joy has never gone away! After I made that discovery as an almost three-year-old, it just got better and better: as I grew, as I aged, as I went and got a teaching degree, as I went to share my knowledge with others and found that there were even more levels of teaching and learning. When I began to work with young children and teach them, and then older children and teach them, and then adults and teach them, the feeling of contentment, joy, and pleasure in purpose just got better and better. I am still enamored with it today. I am still in love with the profession and the houses of knowledge and all that is still available to learn and share.

I didn't realize as a young child that the discovery of what moved me in my life was what uncovered my call, my destiny. There are many who go off to life, and college, and after college, and master's degrees, still wondering about what they should do with their lives, what they should be. But I believe everyone can and does come to that place of discovery at some point in life. I never had a question mark about it from that almost three-year-old to this day. When asked what I want to be when I grow up, the answer was and still is a teacher. I want to be a teacher when I grow up. I believe we all come to that place of discovery. I believe the difference may be that some of us allow the voices and distractions of the world to cloud our vision to the discovery that uncovers. I know for me, it has happened in other areas of my life such as finances, relationships, and seizing opportunities. Thankfully, it is never too late to go back and seek, pray, find, and discover or rediscover to uncover.

That discovery of the love of what moved me helped me to uncover destiny. Once I made the discovery and uncovered the elements of success to carry, walk, and live out the draw and the call associated with the discovery, I went full speed ahead. It *became* my focus. People didn't always understand it. My propensity for success in academia caused many people in my teen years, and later in college, to ask me "why." Why was I "limiting" myself to being a teacher? Why wasn't I studying to be a doctor? Why wasn't I studying to be a political leader? Why wasn't I studying to be a lawyer? Why wasn't I going to be something more? I didn't have an answer that was acceptable to those who asked. However, I knew I had discovered my call. I had discovered my purpose, and I wasn't letting it go. It was too good, too moving, too rewarding, too precious to let go.

I am sure that it is only by God's grace that I was able to discover and uncover that reality at so young an age and never let it go, never be moved by the voices and influences of others who didn't understand it and didn't agree with it. No doubt, had I pursued other fields, I could have been successful. However, I can't imagine finding the same joy in just about anything else. When I discovered and latched on to that truth, that this was for me, this was my destiny, it fueled the necessary success.

Even though there were those who didn't agree with my focus or felt like I should be doing something "better," there was another faction at work as well. Thankfully, there were also those who saw my desire and my pursuit of that discovery, my pursuit of that pleasure, my pursuit of that joy, my pursuit of that destination (destiny). There were some who saw the discovery and nurtured it. They told me how gifted I was at teaching and learning (some before I was able to actively pursue it, some even before high school). I would be told how well I'd explained things to others, even to adults before I *was* one. I would be told how I taught others to do things well. During high school, I was asked to tutor, to share my knowledge, to help others, both children and adults. As a teen, I volunteered for an organization that helped immigrants learn literacy and the English language. As a teen, I helped adults learn to read. Others could see the gift, could see the purpose, could see the destiny (destination).

As a young child, I discovered, and began to uncover, what was destined for my life. Again, this is not the story of most. It's my story. It isn't even my story in all areas of my life, but I found it can work in every area just the same. It is never too late to discover to uncover, to propel us to joy and success in every area of life. It may take longer in some areas than others. It may be a longer process for some than for others. For those who may take a little longer to discover and uncover – perhaps it's later in high school, or in college, or even later than that – rest assured, on this side of heaven, it is never too late.

What holds any of us back from discovering to uncover? I have found that we allow ourselves to be distracted by what others want for us, or what others desire for us, or what others think we should want or desire. I have heard that story many times from people in discovering their purpose, discovering who they are, and discovering their draw and their call. Have you discovered your draw, your purpose, your call? What moves you to joy and to action? Have you allowed yourself to discover the plan and purpose God has for you in your life? Will you purpose to seek, search, pray, ask, and find the joy of discovery of purpose and focus to uncover the drive, resolve, persistence, and commitment necessary to propel you into success?

When we discover, we are then able to begin to uncover the truth of who we are and what we've been called to do and be, what we have been purposed for. That discovery and uncovering impacts not only ourselves, but also the lives of others (Romans 8:19). It's a blessing to them, and empowerment to prosper. If you haven't reached that place, there is always time to get there (Joel 2:25-27). Pray, seek God, ask the One who created us to help bring about that discovery so that you can uncover (Jeremiah 33:3). In discovering and in uncovering, there is great joy (Romans 8:28). There is contentment. There is fulfillment. That is my desire for everyone, and I believe that is our Heavenly Father's desire for us all as well (Deuteronomy 30:19; 3 John 2). May we be able to cultivate young lives so that more of us can discover earlier rather than later, and then uncover throughout our lives, bringing us joy and fulfillment and purpose, helping us to be blessed to be a blessing (Genesis 12:2-3).

POWER POINTS

God says,

"For I know the plans I have for you, says the Lord." (Jeremiah 29:11a NLT)

"Call to me, and I will answer you, and show you great and mighty things, which you do not know." (Jeremiah 33:3 NKJV)

AFFIRMATION

I purpose in my heart and mind to seek, search, pray, ask, and find the joy of discovery. I maintain focus to uncover the drive, resolve, persistence, and commitment necessary to propel me into success. I do so in every area. I am destined and designed with and for specific purpose. I am destined and designed for success in every area of my life. I believe it. I receive it. I achieve it.

CHAPTER 14

DISCOVERY: WHO KNEW
(AND HOW COME THEY NEVER TOLD ME)?

"Moreover whom he did predestinate, them he also called: and whom he called, them he also justified: and whom he justified, them he also glorified." (Romans 8:30 KJV)

"And so those whom God set apart, he called; and those he called, he put right with himself, and he shared his glory with them." (Romans 8:30 GNB)

As a young child, I learned and began to recognize that people will either reward and celebrate you or not. Now, while you have some semblance of control over this, what I did not learn until far later in life was that you don't really have a whole lot of control over whether or not people choose to reward or celebrate you. You can attempt to please people, you can attempt to learn what people's preferences are and what pleases them, but ultimately, it is not possible to please anyone all of the time. It is certainly not possible to please everyone any of the time either.

As a young child, I did have some specific revelations as to was important to me, and what was important to life. Sadly, early in life, I did not learn the lesson of Who to please and how. I did not learn the lesson of making great decisions, no matter who it pleases, until far later in life. With all of the gifts and talents that God had bestowed upon me and saw fit to have nurtured in me by my family and others in my environment, I still had an issue with people pleasing and desiring to be rewarded and celebrated by others. This, in and of itself, is not wrong. However, if that becomes one's driving motivation, I have found that it is the misplaced motives that can make anything wrong. If accolades from others become our focal point, I have found that it taints the deed or action and makes it wrong.

As a young child, I started building a habit of trying to please others. I started a habit of not focusing in on what may have been the right thing or the righteous thing, not focusing in on what I was called to or what I might be held accountable for. Instead, I was focused too often on how to get the next approval, the next smile, the next affirmation, the next confirmation, the next agreement. This is not a good way to live life, and it is not God's way for our lives. I am very glad that I learned that lesson. I often feel like I learned it much too late. Thankfully, all things work together for good, and God is masterful at turning what doesn't look good into something that works for our good (Romans 8:28). So, I encourage you to learn that lesson. If you haven't learned it, I encourage you to take the reflections here, whatever age and stage you are in, and remember that a focus on what is right, what you are called to, and what you are held accountable for should be the main thing.

That focus will keep us in a God focus. It will prevent needless self-criticism and needless cowering to anyone else's wills and preferences and likes, aside from God.

In the end, I want God to be pleased with my life. I feel like it is then that I can be pleased with my life – mistakes, flaws, successes, challenges, and all. I wasn't told that lesson. I wasn't shown that lesson; it wasn't modeled before me. I wasn't given scenarios and examples to role play. I had to learn it, mostly by trial-and-error and hard knocks. This lesson is one thing that I wish had been ingrained into me as a young child.

I was always told I could do anything and be anything I wanted. I was always told that I had success inside of me and that I could allow that to go forth and to come out. I was told that I am somebody destined for greatness and that I can! But I wasn't given the lesson that most of us figure out at some point: the lesson of the flightiness and the futility of trying to please people. Most of us have heard this famous quote, and I pray that we take it to heart daily. I've adjusted it slightly here: "You can please some of the people all of the time; you can please all of the people some of the time; but you can't please all of the people all of the time." Any focus on pleasing people is the wrong focus.

I am not sure if the people around me and the people who influenced me the most had already learned this lesson, but I don't recall anyone ever sharing it with me. Be the boss. Yes. Get ahead. Yes. Be number one. Yes. Be on top. Yes. Those were all lessons that were drilled into me by others, by influencers in my life. No one really homed in on an understanding of remaining focused:

obtaining and maintaining a focus on what is really important. It seemed like applause, awards, and accolades were the most important things, or at least very high on the list of importance.

So, I'm not sure who already knew that lesson as I traveled the path to learning it myself. I do know that I did not hear it taught along the way. I remember how, once I came to that realization, I wondered why I'd never heard anyone else say that, teach that, drill that in along the way. I'm not sure who all knew or when they knew. I just felt a bit cheated and slighted because I felt like others must have known but nobody ever told me. It seemed I had to come to that realization and learn that lesson all on my own. So, I share the lesson with you. This is what I've found, and it's one of my endeavors to share it with whomever I can, with whomever will hear it, with whomever will take the lesson to heart in today's world of likes and views and follows and subscribes. It's important to maintain focus on what really matters.

Any focus on getting others to affirm you is the wrong focus. Learn who *you* are, learn who *you* have been called to be, allow God to affirm that, and then affirm it yourself. Allow God to confirm that, and then confirm it yourself. Rehearse the affirmations necessary to keep the focus on fulfilling your life's call and purpose; what you've been created and ordained to do and to be; and who you have been created and ordained to influence, minister to, and serve. There's a blessing in that lesson. I believe there is an even greater blessing in learning it sooner rather than later.

What will you choose to focus in on? Will it be the flightiness of people? Will it be their affirmations and likes? Or will it be your

God-given purpose and call? Will you apply the affirmations of being able to do and be whatever you're called to do and be? Will your choice be to live out the greatness inside you already, being equipped with exactly what you need and surrounded with exactly who you need at every specific time that you have a need? Will you recognize and focus in on the people and the resources to cultivate who you have ultimately been called to be, who you have ultimately been purposed to be, and who you have ultimately been designed to serve? May we learn and apply this lesson sooner rather than later.

POWER POINTS

God says,

"We ought to obey God rather than men." (Acts 5:29b KJV)

"And whatsoever ye do, do it heartily, as to the Lord, and not unto men." (Colossians 3:23 KJV)

AFFIRMATION

I have been designed, chosen, and called for specific greatness and assignment in the earth. I am uniquely chosen and designed by God for my assignment. Regardless of who affirms, confirms, likes, or agrees with my God-given purpose, I am charged with and committed to living it out to the fullest in every area of my life. I choose to affirm the fulfillment of the assignment given me as God affirms me. I choose to confirm the assignment and my commitment to its completion and fulfillment as God confirms me. I choose to find and take joy in the commitment to and fulfillment of my assignment as God provides the divine connections, resources, prosperity, and productivity I need to fulfill it. I am not and will not be led, influenced, or deterred by the opinions of people in opposition to the completion and fulfillment of my God-given purpose. I rise to the occasion of maintaining focus on fulfillment and the joy and satisfaction that come with it.

Alone in the Crowd

Alone in the Crowd

This final section reflects on the lessons during the transition of childhood. It reflects on the shift from wonder and excitement about the world around us to noticing our place in it. It is often during this season of life that we begin to notice others around us and how we may be alike or different. It is often in this season of life that we begin to question how and where we fit. Though it is often only in looking back, it is also in this time that we see patterns in our lives: patterns of behavior, patterns of preferences, patterns of influence, patterns of action. If we look deeper into the make-up of those patterns in our lives, we will see God at work. We will see God's workings in our foreground and our background, to guide us to the answer to that question of belonging, fit, and purpose. *If* (and when) we attend to noticing, identifying, and recognizing God at work, we see His work all the more. In this season, we may not know what it's called, but looking back, it has been there all along. May we look for, attend to, notice, identify, and recognize His work in us and for us. May that attentiveness propel us into purpose and destiny!

CHAPTER 15

ONLY CHILD

"Each person is given something to do that shows who God is: Everyone gets in on it, everyone benefits." (1 Corinthians 12:7 MSG)

I am an only child – the only child of my father and my mother's union. I also have eighteen younger siblings. Yes, I am an only child with eighteen siblings. None of those eighteen younger siblings, fourteen of whom I grew up with, have the exact same parentage as I. I am the first and the last of my parents' union and therefore distinctly unique, an only child.

This unique distinction was always quite apparent when I was growing up, as there are three years between me and the first of my siblings. The years extend all the way to thirty between me and the last. In every way possible, my position and standing in the family, as both an only child and the eldest of eighteen siblings, is unique in the world. Not just in my neighborhood, not just in my city, not just in my state, not just in my country – in the world.

This, it might seem, should have given me some clue that I would never quite be considered the "norm" by anyone's standards, not that I believe there is such a thing as normal. Registering far out of the norm leaves me an outlier among most households. For the most part, statistically speaking, I am probably an anomaly.

It seems to be human nature to be a part of, to have, and to build community; I believe most or all of us have an innate desire to identify with others, to identify with something, to belong, to be a part. At times, circumstances and situations can cloud our vision to the important things to which we belong: our families, our communities, our schools, our churches, our faiths, our workplaces, our professions. There may be times when the ways that we stand out or do not identify with others, the things that make us unique, can also make us feel less than a part of a community. There are times or circumstances in life that can make one feel very solo (often leading to feeling "so low"). One feels like an only, a stand-out-never-fit-in only. I don't believe that there's much validity in such feelings, but the feelings exist, nevertheless. Our uniqueness and failure to fit may bring about feelings of inadequacy and discouragement.

There were many times in my life growing up when I did not feel a part of any community. I didn't quite connect with my family, my school, my community, my neighborhood. I was an outlier in most ways possible. The nature of children can be a bit cruel in pointing that out. No doubt it is in an effort to make themselves feel more a part and less of an outlier. Nevertheless, there's a certain sting to not being a part, to being singled out and called out, an only child.

I did not grow up with the benefits of the atmosphere of an only child: not having to share toys, having my parent or parents all to myself, and other such things. I did not have the benefit of always feeling a part of my communities. I was, however, able to recognize and take joy in some of the benefits that I *did* have. There was always a hustle and bustle about our house after my third year of life, so I never had a feeling of loneliness. I grew up with amazing people who taught me to love everyone gently, kindly, and patiently, and to see value in them all; to notice gifts and talents in everyone. Now, had I truly been an only child with no other siblings and only my parents to connect to at home (perhaps some extended family members too), I may not have been able to develop the necessary skills to interact with all manner of people, which helps me in my faith, in ministry, and professionally.

Those life lessons on people skills, how to love everyone, and how to enjoy the hustle and bustle have been invaluable. Being very distinct and unique, and therefore being able to identify with those who may have the feelings of standing out and being an only in a community, has also been invaluable. Those life lessons and experiences have helped me to live out and walk out my destiny. I knew from a young age that I was called to serve others and to help whomever I could, whenever I could. Being an only child while also being part of a huge, blended family helped me to cultivate the necessary characteristics, values, and mindsets that afford me success in my encounters with others, success in accepting people for who they are and where they are and helping them to learn and grow. The skills and experiences that come from my life have helped me to be exactly who I needed to be to fulfill my God-gifted calling and purpose in the earth: in my family, in my schools, in my neighborhood, in my community, in my city, in my state, in my country, in the world.

While, statistically, there is probably an exceedingly small percentage of people with any type of similar background, my uniqueness has benefited me. I can see in so many ways how being just who God created me to be and situated me to be, has afforded me everything I need to be exactly who He has designed and destined for me to be. I think that realization, that revelation, is also invaluable. I think that kind of revelation is what most are searching for in life. How do I fit? What do I have to contribute? How can I live prosperously and contentedly and joyfully amidst everyone else? How can I share that prosperity and joy and contentment?

For a short span of time, the behavior of others caused me to wish for something different, for something that I perceived as more normal, for something that would help me to fit in, for something that would alleviate my standing out. When I was a child amid the teasing and ridicule of some of the other children, and even a few adults, I wished for something different.

I came to the realization that I loved my family (all of it), that I enjoyed my life (most of it), and that there was not much I could do to change either; this helped me to enjoy the benefits of both and to see them as positive assets with definite benefits. I came to the realization that I could be okay. I could be happy with what I had and take joy in it. Sure, I could always work toward improvements where appropriate, but I was okay with what I had. I was okay with the plans that I had to go forward to make things better for me, for my family, for my communities. I learned to become okay with the teasing or the inconsiderate remarks and implications. I learned to be okay with my uniqueness. Those lessons and that resolve took me to another place of contentedness (Philippians 4:11), content with exactly who I was, exactly the family I'd been given and blessed with. I was able to rest assured that I was blessed with everything that I needed to live a good, happy, and complete life.

What is your resolve? What is your revelation? Will you spend your life wishing for something different, hoping to hide or change who you really are or where you've come from? I challenge us to use our backgrounds and our experiences and our lives to aid and assist us, even to launch us into fulfilling the plan and purpose that we've been given in our families, in our neighborhoods, in our communities, in our towns, in our cities, in our states, in our provinces, in our countries, in our world. Will you rise to the challenge?

POWER POINTS

God says,

"Not that I speak in respect of want: for I have learned, in whatsoever state I am, therewith to be content." (Philippians 4:11 KJV)

AFFIRMATION

I have been gifted the life connections and experiences that make me who I am. I choose to use every experience and connection to my benefit. I choose to make the choices that use every experience as a step toward my destiny, my call, and my purpose. Even if I feel alone, solo, or only, I will remember that I am unique *and* I am part of communities that need me to contribute my uniqueness. I choose to strive for better in all areas of my life *while* being content with the progress I have already made. I am content to continue to learn the lessons necessary for me to contribute in the best ways possible to the communities in which I belong and serve.

CHAPTER 16

SILENCE IS GOLDEN

"But Jesus held his peace." (Matthew 26:63b KJV)

"... but he answered nothing." (Mark 15:3b KJV)

As a child, when I was around people other than my family, I did far more listening and observing than initiating conversations and talking. My family was rather nomadic, so I was in a continuous state of attempting to fit into places and people groups with a chameleon-like blending. While I wouldn't call myself shy, one could say I was comfortable keeping to myself and being in the background or on the sidelines. Today the terminology might be "introvert." Observation and blending were good ways to scope out the lay of the land in new environments and with unfamiliar people. It is easier to put a foot in an open mouth than a closed one.

My quietness and silence were often efforts to find some sort of commonality and some level of comfort. New environments and new people were not easy for me to read in order to know how to respond. It was hard to tell what I should or shouldn't do in situations with new neighborhoods, new neighbors, new teachers, new classmates.

I felt a need to find some way to fit into new environments and to fit in with the people there. I was never sure if my authentic self would be acceptable to a new group, or if I might be ostracized or called out because I was new or did not fit into the already established communities.

I remained quiet or silent to allow myself time to study the new environments and the new people. I found that this gave me that time to study and figure out behavior that could gain me enough acceptance to become more comfortable and feel less like an outsider. This strategy worked almost all of the time.

I discovered there was another benefit to silence. As a child, it often made adults view me in a better light. Teachers, neighbors, distant family members, and the like would categorize me as "good" if I was quiet or silent. Positive comments would be made alluding to the assumption that I must be well-behaved, pleasant, and smart since I was quiet. I'll not refute any of those descriptors (though Mommy might have a comment or two to add), but they were assumptions nevertheless. Often before I was comfortable enough to be my authentic self around those adults, they would already have formed some opinion of me based upon those positive descriptors that came from my displays of silence and quietness.

In my faith walk, I have learned that there is another twist on the benefit of silence. Jesus Himself set a fine example of this use of silence. When interrogated and (falsely) accused, when challenged on His identity, Jesus remained silent (Matthew 26:63; Mark 15:3). Initially, I wondered why. Why not speak up? Why not defend Yourself? I learned this key: there is no need to justify Truth. Jesus was assured of His identity and every action that He took. He knew exactly who He was, His purpose, the plan for His life, and the completion of His mission. He had nothing to prove any further than He had already proven.

My takeaway from Jesus's example was to become secure in my own identity. God created me for a specific purpose. He has a plan for my life and a special calling just for me. God has wired and equipped me for that specific plan and purpose. He has made me unique and provided me with unique experiences and inclinations to fulfill that plan and purpose to which He has called me. When I am secure in who God has created me to be and what He has called me to do, I do not have to answer to those who want me to justify my identity and call, to turn away from it, or to abandon it. I need not feel obligated to convince anyone who would rather have me believe otherwise.

It is my right and responsibility to learn and discover God's call on my life. Once I make the discovery, I can listen and observe in order to learn to become secure in the call. I can become comfortable with my preparation for answering that call. I can be responsible to the call and to those who wait for me to fulfill it (Romans 8:19). I can have an assurance that gives me a quiet peace, a silence of knowing.

It is my right and responsibility to carry out the plan and purpose God has for my life. Once I know His plan and purpose which has been designated specifically to me, I can be secure in that plan and purpose, the one laid out just for me by the God of the universe. Who could possibly know better how to orchestrate my life than my Faithful Heavenly Father? I can be secure in the provision He has made for my special plan and purpose and remain focused in seeing it through. I can become comfortable and content in this knowledge without a need to convince others to believe the same. I can allow my life and what God accomplishes through me to be the necessary evidence to speak for me.

What about you? Are you secure in your God-given identity, His call upon your life? Have you answered the call? Are you secure in the plan and purpose God has established for your life? Have you discovered and learned what that plan is and what it entails? Will you allow God to use the experiences of your life to fulfill that plan and purpose? Do you still feel obligated to answer those who want you to justify your identity and call, or to turn away from it, or to abandon it?

If you have any question about God's specific call, plan, and purpose for your life, who better to ask than God Himself? He promises to answer (Jeremiah 33:3). Be ready to be quiet, to listen, and to observe. Know that if you have not already found it, a security awaits you in the response that will be given in the quiet (1 Kings 19:12). An assurance awaits you that will empower you to be secure in who you are in Him. Then there will be no need to answer to justify your identity. You can allow what God will do through you to speak on your behalf.

POWER POINTS

God says,

"... but let it be [the inner beauty of] the hidden person of the heart, with the imperishable quality and unfading charm of a gentle and peaceful spirit [one that is calm and self-controlled, not overanxious, but serene and spiritually mature] which is very precious in the sight of God." (1 Peter 3:4 AMP)

"Wherefore, my beloved brethren, let every man be swift to hear, slow to speak, slow to wrath..." (James 1:19 KJV)

AFFIRMATION

I am called by God. God has a specific plan and purpose for my life. I can rest assured in the plan God has for me. God has promised to answer when I inquire. I am secure in the plan and purpose God has for my life. God's plan for me is revealed, and I agree and align with His plan. I am quick to hear, listen, and observe. I am slow to speak, and I keep a quiet spirit. God justifies me. I allow God's work in me and through me to speak on my behalf, proving who I am in Him.

CHAPTER 17

NO ONE IS AN ISLAND

"Then shall ye call upon me, and ye shall go and pray unto me, and I will hearken unto you." (Jeremiah 29:12 KJV)

In the earliest years of my life, I existed in a sort of a bubble. I did not have many encounters with others that didn't include my family. My view of the world was a bit skewed. We lived with or very close to family all of my early years. I had either cousins or siblings around all the time, sometimes both. I didn't know anyone who was an only child (without extended family to hang with regularly) until I was around eight years old. While I loved my siblings and extended family dearly, I don't know that I truly gained an appreciation for them until I met someone who had none.

Around age eight, I attended a different school from all of my younger school-age siblings at the time, being three or more years older than them. One of the girls from that class befriended me, and Mommy allowed me to hang out at her house for homework time after school.

My friend was my same age. She lived in the penthouse of a high-rise in our neighborhood a few blocks from my apartment home. She was a latchkey kid, and most times her parents were not home when we arrived. She would check in with the doorman of her building when we arrived. The doorman would exchange greetings with us and let us up to her home in the penthouse elevator.

It was a beautiful home, and I was initially amazed at the spaciousness. She was an only child and was the only one at home, aside from a domestic worker who was at her beck and call for snacks, help, questions, etc. It was a bit of culture shock for me, but lots of fun. It seemed like she had it so good. She had all of that to herself.

As we began to make this a daily habit after school, I began to notice that she did not want me to leave after completing homework. She would ask me to stay longer and longer, later and later. She began asking me if I could call my mom and ask to stay longer. Initially, I thought nothing of it. Friends like to hang out. But as Mommy began to enforce the expected time for me to be home, my friend would request for me to push against the restrictions imposed.

When I explained to her the danger of not complying with the rules, namely my punishment and the possibility that I would no longer be able to come over, she revealed the reason she was putting on the peer pressure. She was lonely. Without my presence, she would be alone in her big, plush house, with no other children to talk or play with. I discovered her parents would not let her visit other kids at their homes, despite allowing one friend to come to the penthouse after school.

That stuck with me. I was able to go home with Mommy and my siblings waiting there. I had someone to play with all the time. Even when we sometimes irritated one another, I never would have wanted to be home alone with no other kids around. I had never thought about that before. I never knew there were lonely kids who did not have other kids to play with. I never realized how blessed I was to share the fun, learning, and family with my siblings. I could not imagine having to come home to loneliness. I could not imagine coming home to emptiness. I could not imagine coming home to many, many things and so much space with no people to fill the space. I felt it was sad.

In my faith walk, I learned that I did something similar with God's presence. God is omnipresent, everywhere at the same time. He has always been with me. He knows me. He knew me even before I was born (Ephesians 1:4). But I spent far too much time not recognizing the blessing and benefits of His presence and His love for me. I spent too much time taking God's presence and help for granted. True, I was ignorant to His presence in the beginning, but after coming into the knowledge of God's perpetual presence, I did not properly appreciate it. I have the Maker of the universe as my Faithful Father and my Ally. I never have to worry about being alone without Him or about lacking provision and all that I need. I have the privilege and benefit of being able to call on Him whenever I need, to make inquiries when I need answers or clarity. I have since learned to stay linked to Father God, to continuously acknowledge His presence, to stay plugged in to His power.

Those who do not have a relationship with Father God do not have the benefit of tapping into the presence and power of Almighty God. Ignorance or improper appreciation can limit access to all God is and to all He has. Limited access can result in failure to recognize what is available. Once relationship is established, it is important to recognize the benefits that it activates. Relationship allows one to tap in, to plug in, to stay linked.

Have you established your relationship with Father God and connected to His perpetual presence? He is always there waiting to connect (Revelation 3:20; 1 Kings 8:57). If you have not, take the opportunity to do so now, so that you will no longer take advantage of His perpetual presence. If you have, tap in, stay connected, stay linked. Recognize, act upon, and appreciate the benefits of the relationship.

POWER POINTS

God says,

"*... and, lo, I am with you always, even unto the end of the world. Amen.*" (Matthew 28:20 KJV)

"*Call to Me, and I will answer you, and show you great and mighty things, which you do not know.*" (Jeremiah 33:3 NKJV)

AFFIRMATION

I have the benefit of God's perpetual presence. I am not alone. God is with me always. I stay connected to God and do not take His presence for granted. God hears me when I pray. God answers when I call. I have access to the presence and power of Almighty God, and I tap in. Therefore, I have God's divine presence and power to accomplish all things!

CHAPTER 18

CREEPY CRAWLIES

"It is better to trust in the Lord than to put confidence in man." (Psalm 118:8 KJV)

When I was a little girl, in my early years, a sudden and mysterious nighttime ailment came upon me. There did not seem to be a known cause or related issue to explain the phenomenon. I would experience the sensation of little creatures crawling all over my skin, mostly on my arms and legs. At the time of the initial occurrences, I had no idea what was going on, but would call out to my mommy from bed and explain that there were things crawling on me, creepy crawlies. Mommy would get me up and out of bed and investigate me and the linens, which would turn up nothing. This disrupted our nightly routine, which was to bathe, brush teeth, don a nightgown, get into bed for the nightly bedtime story, then lights out until the morning.

I am not sure what triggered or initiated the creepy crawlies – that was my only way of describing the ailment with my limited vocabulary. The situation was highly uncomfortable. I have no doubt that Mommy was eventually at her wit's end. So, after quite a few nights of this with no seeming resolution or relief, Mommy would wipe me down at each complaint, investigate the bed, investigate my skin, and put me back to bed. I'm not sure if she fully believed me after continually finding no evidence of a cause. After continued complaints, we finally went to the doctor. The doctors couldn't find anything either, so they sent Mommy home with an idea of some remedies and tests to do, to investigate my description of the ailment. All the tests came out negative. All of the specimens and samples that I was called to produce turned up nothing.

Finally, after months of this, one doctor had some kind of epiphany and gave my mother a prescription for a rather expensive topical moisturizing cream, with instructions to slather me down before bed and to report back how it worked. Mommy did. And it worked! According to that doctor, it turned out that my skin was dry. This was the culprit of the creepy crawlies. Once moisturized after my bath, I didn't seem to have any more issues with creepy crawlies.

All the ineffective tests, the time spent, the efforts, and the long nights for my mommy were remedied by a moisturizing cream. Sometimes answers and solutions are simple but potentially complicated to find. Who knew that dry skin could give you the sensation of critters crawling all over you? The words I had to describe the ailment to Mommy were not helpful in determining a cause or solution. She hadn't had her own personal experience with the same thing and so was not able to help me. Most of the doctors we visited seemed to have no clue either, until a remedy finally came about after testing out lots of potential remedies that had yielded no solution.

Life can be like that. Sometimes a solution and an answer can be close at hand but not easily recognized. One can take many complex steps, trials, and remedies to finally come to the conclusion of the matter by finding a solution. As much as others may try, they cannot identify with the experience or help with the solution. It all comes down to one who knows how to remedy the issue.

I have found that God is all knowing, all seeing, and ever present. He has every answer and every solution. I have also found, however, that if I do not position myself to ask the right questions in the right way and to prepare for the answer, then I spend more time awaiting a solution that was available the entire time. If I don't tune in to listen once I've asked to receive that solution, or if I don't believe that He will hear and answer me, I can go through some very complex and complicated steps (like going to all the useless doctors and doing the ineffective tests) to get what was ultimately pretty simple.

I experience joy and relief when I take my issues, my problems, and my inquiries to God. God hears me and answers. I apply His solution, and things work out on my behalf. Sometimes the process is not quick. Sometimes it's a journey of getting to the place where I listen and apply the remedy. I stop, inquire, listen and hear, then apply His solution.

Learning that God's ear and help are available and learning the steps to stop, inquire, listen, hear, and apply has helped me to come to solutions more quickly. Earlier in life, far too many times, that process was more complicated and drawn out. Like the back and forth between the doctors and tests that yielded no remedy, the process was more complicated before I knew what to do. I had to go to the Source for the answer, await the instruction to remedy the issue, and then apply the solution. Once I knew what to do, I experienced the joy and contentment of having found the answer and applying it.

I invite you to cut down the time along the journey of finding a necessary remedy for every issue. I invite you to build the habit of going to God first as the Source of remedy and solution. I challenge you to go to God first and then to stop, listen, and apply His remedy. Apply the remedy of the all-seeing, all-knowing, all-powerful, ever-present, Faithful Father, whose desire it is to heal, help, and provide for us. Have you tried that process? Have you given Him the opportunity to hear and remedy your issue? Have you stopped to listen and hear what His remedy would be? Have you taken the opportunity and the time to apply His remedy? Allow His remedy to alleviate your issue and to bring your solution. No more creepy crawlies. I invite you to practice this today and every day going forward. It can make for such a simpler life and for such blessed assurance. Try it. Make it a habit. Take joy in it. Build confidence in this process and allow it to transform your life.

POWER POINTS

God says,

"And this is the confidence that we have in him, that, if we ask any thing according to his will, he heareth us: and if we know that he hear us, whatsoever we ask, we know that we have the petitions that we desired of him." (1 John 5:14-15 KJV)

"And I say unto you, Ask, and it shall be given you; seek, and ye shall find; knock, and it shall be opened unto you. For every one that asketh receiveth; and he that seeketh findeth; and to him that knocketh it shall be opened." (Luke 11:9-10 KJV)

AFFIRMATION

God hears me when I go to Him in prayer. I have been given the opportunity and the right, as His child, to go to Him in prayer, asking, seeking, and knocking for the remedy to every issue. God hears me and He answers. I take time to stop, be still, quiet the external and internal noise and hear God's answer and remedy for my every issue. God honors my submission and provides me with all I need to address every issue. I patiently build the necessary skills to hear and obey God's guidance. I take the answers given by God and apply them in joyful obedience. Thank you, God, for Your loving solutions to my every need.

CHAPTER 19

PTOSIS

"For I will restore ... because they called thee an Outcast, saying, This is Zion, whom no man seeketh after." (Jeremiah 30:17 KJV)

For as long as I can remember, I have been the sort of person whose thoughts and ideas about the world have been noticeably different from others. My actions in situations tend to be atypical. Quite often, explaining my thoughts, ideas, actions, and logic to others receives a less-than-enthusiastic response from most, and many times questioning glances and stares.

The time of discovering my invisible peculiarities in thought, character, and action was preceded by a visible peculiarity. A congenital disorder affected my face and does so to this day, to a minor degree. Not as many people ask about the disorder today as when I was a child. People tend to be much more forward with a child, especially other children. Peers tended to be very vocal about this physical peculiarity, even mean on occasion.

When I was a child, people seemed to find the physical disorder to be a fascinating anomaly about which to inquire, observe, and study. This public fascination made me very uncomfortable. The physical disorder made me stand out, but not in a good way. It took me some time to learn that the response and reactions of others did not mean that there was something wrong with me. I had to learn that I had control over my level of comfort. I could choose to be uncomfortable with other people's responses and reactions, or I could choose not to be.

Each person is a unique individual. The outer physical appearance could be the most aesthetically pleasing to others; however, it is what's on the inside that has the most value. But that is not what people see first. Sight can be a powerful influencer, though not always an accurate or trustworthy one, hence the well-known quotes such as "Seeing is believing," "You can't judge a book by its cover," "All that glitters isn't gold," "Your eyes are playing tricks on you" – and *"For we walk by faith, not by sight"* (2 Corinthians 5:7).

It can be a challenge to overcome the obstacles presented by the lack of control over anyone else's response to your outer appearance. Identifying those who are able to set aside the outer appearance for what is to be found on the inside is not an easy task either. There are definite benefits to being able to dismiss those who are not able to allow mindset, motive, and character to supersede outward appearance. Yet the uncomfortable stings of being visibly different and the responses to that difference are not lessened by this ability.

There is value in individuality and the things that make people unique, even though, when the outstanding characteristics are visible ones, when the uniqueness is more evident on the outside, the response to it can be less than positive. Without the understanding that everyone is created differently and that it's okay to be different, I may miss the value of going beyond what is seen. God does that. He goes beyond what others can see. He gets to the heart of the matter, the heart of a person. He acknowledges that we judge on the outside while He looks at what is inside (1 Samuel 16:7). He also acknowledges that what is on the inside, in the heart, is what drives a person's words, actions, character, and motives (Matthew 12:34; Luke 6:45).

The physical disorder remains outwardly evident for me. It still draws negative attention sometimes. But I am not made as uncomfortable by the reactions of others any longer. I have grown to recognize that I cannot control anyone else's reactions. How they respond to my outward appearance has little to do with me. How I allow their responses and reactions to impact me, on the other hand, has everything to do with me. I have chosen to become secure and confident with what God says of me and with maintaining a mindset, motives, and character in alignment with what God says of me. I recognize the greater value of what is inside a person (including myself) and strive to live accordingly.

We each have own our journey to accepting who we are. It helps to have people in our lives who will help us navigate the journey of self-acceptance. We can come to a place where we are content and satisfied without being arrogant, simply being confident in our individuality and uniqueness. For some of us, the journey takes longer than for others, but that's okay. The length of the journey is also a part of our individuality. The journey is worth it and successful as long as we make it there. It is my hope to help get us to that journey, if not to successfully complete it.

What will you decide? Will you allow the responses and reactions of others to influence you and how you respond and react? Will you allow others to determine your level of comfort with who you are and who God has created you to be? Will you decide to search past outward appearances to inner mindsets, motives, and character? Will you decide to allow your own mindsets, motives, and character (your heart) to align with what God says? There is security and confidence in choosing to recognize the greater value.

POWER POINTS

God says,

"... for the Lord seeth not as man seeth; for man looketh on the outward appearance, but the Lord looketh on the heart."
(1 Samuel 16:7b KJV)

AFFIRMATION

I believe what God says about me. I *only* believe what God says about me. I choose to see as God sees. I will not be influenced or moved by sight. I choose to align with God's Word and with His character. I am not moved by the responses and reactions of others. I align my mindset, my actions, my motives, and my character with the Word and the heart of God. I have a heart after God that demonstrates my love for Him and that demonstrates His love to others.

CHAPTER 20

HELP IS NOT INDIVIDUAL NOR ONE-SIDED

"Knowing that whatsoever good thing any man doeth, the same shall he receive of the Lord..." (Ephesians 6:8 KJV)

One of the wonderful things about growing up as a kid with multiple siblings is that help is available for most endeavors. There is help to make messes and to clean them up, help to get into trouble and to get out of it, help to play games and make memories, help to enjoy life and to share parents, help to make and share funny stories, help to share comfort and tragedy, help to overcome fears and to share life in general.

Growing up with siblings, sometimes strengths and weaknesses can balance out. One sibling may be good at something that supports a weak area in one or more of the others. The reverse may also be true, as the sharing among siblings is on both ends. Siblings volley between being the recipient and the giver. It can be lopsided at times, but everyone plays a part. Things often have a way of balancing out. I would not trade any of the time I had to grow with my siblings learning this symbiotic relationship. It was a wonderfully fulfilling period in life. The benefits are wondrous and excellent, as each does their part working together conjointly with one another to accomplish goals, to accomplish tasks, to accomplish life – to accomplish.

As I began to grow in faith, I began to learn that this is true for the body of Christ too. The Bible describes it as many members making up one body, likening it to our human body and how every part is needed, is useful, and has a specific purpose (1 Corinthians 12). All of the individual parts are distinct. No part has the same function as another, at least not as effectively: eyes, ears, nose, feet, fingers, thumbs, all parts have a purpose and work together.

Each member has a place. Each member has strengths. Each member has been called to a specific work. Just as the eye does not need to be envious of the ear because they each have a specific role, the same is true of the body of Christ. Each member has a specific role distinct from any other but connected and working best together with one another. Different does not mean better, but different also does not mean worse. Different simply means that there is an established purpose for each one. The eye can be secure and content operating in its visual gift. The ear can be secure and content operating in its auditory gift. The nose can be secure and content operating in its olfactory gift. The same is true in the body of Christ. I can be content doing my part and being exactly who I am and who I have been created to be.

Like siblings (as we are God's children), all the members of the body of Christ are connected. Each individual member is connected to the many, to the body, to the others in the family, each helping and supporting one another together. The eye can not carry out the mission of the body alone; indeed, no individual members of the body can carry out its mission alone. The body works best and most optimally when all the parts, all the members, work together, supporting each individual strength to carry out the mission. I am connected to others in the body of Christ to support each individual strength to carry out tasks and missions and goals. The beautiful symbiotic nature of humankind mirrors God's purpose and plan for those of us who walk by Faith (2 Corinthians 5:7).

Have you found your place in the family of Faith? Are you contributing your strengths and gifts to the family while supporting the strengths of the other members and being supported yourself? Will you add your individualism and be connected to the others to carry out the tasks, missions, and goals? You have been called and equipped to do so. Join us if you have not already. If you are already a part of the whole, be supported by us for the optimum function.

POWER POINTS

God says,

"Wherefore comfort yourselves together, and edify one another, even as also ye do." (1 Thessalonians 5:11 KJV)

"Two are better than one; because they have a good reward for their labor." (Ecclesiastes 4:9 NKJV)

AFFIRMATION

I am called and equipped by God to be a part of His family. I am a member of the body of Christ. I join my God-given gifts and talents to the individual members of the body of Christ so that we support one another in being strong, edified, helped, supported, and rewarded. I am the unique individual God has created me to be. I connect my unique individualism to the other members of the body of Christ to complete the work of God in unity, in excellence, and in strength.

CHAPTER 21

CHEW AND SERVE

"I have fed you with milk, and not with meat: for hitherto ye were not able to bear it, neither yet now are ye able." (1 Corinthians 3:2 KJV)

"… and are become such as have need of milk, and not of strong meat." (Hebrews 5:12b KJV)

When I was a young child, as the family grew, so did our exposure to the ways and needs of babies. This was before the time of mechanical food processors and baby food makers. In our family, once an infant grew past the stage of taking only milk and required further substantive nutrition, there needed to be dietary adjustments. Finances that could have been used for the purchase of baby food – the limited selection available at the time – were better spent on other necessities. Thus, we had Mommy's solution to meet the need. For any table food that could not be softened, mashed, and liquified, Mommy would first masticate those stronger food items that the toothless toddler would be unable to digest and proceed to feed them in small quantities to the baby, in mama bird fashion.

This was a norm in our house for many consecutive births. We thought nothing of it. Until the babes could chew and digest table food on their own, there had to be some sort of transition between their former diet of solely milk and the ability to properly access the table food. The milk no longer sufficed to fully satisfy the nutritional needs of the little ones after a time. As their bodies began to mature and grow, there was an "in between" stage of need. They did not yet have the full growth to enable them to access the same as the older members of the family.

God describes this same phenomenon in His Word. The Bible gives us a spiritual account of the same growth pattern, a description of going from milk to meat. It describes how, when we start off in our faith walk, we start off needing the lightweight, sufficient spiritual nutrition of milk. When we mature, we are expected to grow towards being able to digest stronger spiritual content, especially once the lightweight spiritual nutrition will no longer satisfy the need.

Were a babe to continue to try to grow only on milk for an extended period of time, it would be malnourished. In the same way, if newborn Christians continue only on milk for long periods of time, the same is spiritually true. A person of faith who continues solely on milk is spiritually malnourished. They will eventually be in need of meat.

As I have grown into spiritual maturity, I am grateful for the mastication of the spiritual meat that I was not yet able to fully digest on my own. There have been pastors, my mommy, Sunday school teachers, confirmation classes, conferences, small group communities, Bible classes, and various other entities who have helped me to spiritually digest what I could not have on my own.

As I look back over the time of my faith walk, I can see where God provided the milk I needed. I can also see where He provided a "chew and serve" spiritual nutrition for me while I was growing into spiritual maturity, before I was truly able to digest spiritual meat independently. I am grateful that I have the spiritual nutrition of the meat and am now able to independently digest it. I am also grateful for the opportunities that God now gives me to provide spiritual milk to infants in the faith. I am grateful for those in the Faith who are transitioning and growing, and for how God allows me to chew and serve for them. I am grateful for opportunities to provide meat for the spiritually mature as well.

Where do you fall in your spiritual growth and maturity? Are you holding on to the milk stage a little bit longer than you should, experiencing malnutrition? Are you allowing others to chew and serve where you are unable to digest the meat of God's word and His principles? Are you fully spiritually mature and able to digest the meat? If you fall into the first two categories, take time to thank God for those who provide the spiritual nutrition that you need in whichever form. That spiritual nutrition will help you to grow to the place where you're mature enough to digest spiritual meat. If you fall into the latter category and are able to digest the spiritual meat, consider providing the milk for those who are in need of more basic spiritual nutrition. Consider chewing and serving for those who are in the transition of spiritual growth and maturity, for whom milk will no longer suffice, but who are not yet quite fully able to digest the meat.

POWER POINTS

God says,

"But grow in grace, and in the knowledge of our Lord and Saviour Jesus Christ. To Him be glory both now and for ever. Amen." (2 Peter 3:18 KJV)

"That ye might walk worthy of the Lord unto all pleasing, being fruitful in every good work, and increasing in the knowledge of God…" (Colossians 1:10 KJV)

AFFIRMATION

As a child of God, I grow and mature spiritually. Father God has just the right spiritual food available for me at every stage of my spiritual growth. He provides just the right feeders and materials for me to grow and mature well. I trust every stage He takes me through. I trust that every spiritual nutrient is provided by my Faithful Heavenly Father to ensure that I am nurtured so that I will grow strong enough to help others to mature spiritually. Thank you, Father, for my spiritual growth and maturity!

CONCLUSION

I have reached the end of this portion of this collection. The twenty-one life lessons compiled here represent my early years and the early lessons I have been blessed to learn. I share them with the expectation that your arsenal is now twenty-one weapons richer against the onslaught of self-doubt, discouragement, disillusionment, disenchantment, discount, and defeat. I pray not only that you find the lessons useful, but that you will use and reuse them to affirm what God says. If you find the collection beneficial, share it with others. You are blessed to be a blessing (Genesis 12:3).

Remember to continually activate your faith. Without faith, it is impossible to please God (Hebrews 11:6). Remember to continually meditate on the power points that most relate to you and to both personalize and vocalize the affirmations often. Words have power! What we speak, we hear. Faith comes by hearing, and hearing, and hearing (Romans 10:17). What we hear often enough, we believe. What we believe, we act upon. What we act upon, we manifest. Go forth and work the Word. The Word works if you work it

(Mark 11:23). Speak life! Transform your thinking. Transform your believing. Transform your speaking. Transform your achieving.

The lessons in this collection have served as foundational truths and affirmations – the basics. There are more lessons to come. The lessons learned during my years of salvation and Christian growth and maturity will be compiled in the next volume. There is more to go and more to grow. I conclude the matter for now. May this collection serve you well until the next.

SALVATION AND RESTORATION PRAYER

If you have not yet joined our Faith family, you are invited! For any who are already in the family of God, but may need the relationship restored, you, too, are invited! God loves and cherishes us more than we know. Come join us in building your relationship, or in rebuilding your relationship with Faithful Father God!

I encourage you to go to God in prayer with your own words and ask to join the family, or for restoration in the family. However, if you need help with the words to say, here are some to get you started. I encourage you to pray also for a group of believers with which to connect, regularly, to strengthen your faith and your walk with God. Pray also for the spiritual leaders you need God to send to you.

PRAYER

Father God, I thank you for Your love. Thank You for loving me so much that You sent Jesus to live a life of example for me and to die for my sin. I believe Your Word. I believe that Jesus died to rid me of my sin problem, giving me the right to be adopted into your family just as if I had never sinned. I believe that Jesus rose from the dead and is alive forever, praying for me and answering my prayers. I believe that Jesus sent Your Holy Spirit into the earth to give me the power, comfort, and strategy I need to fulfill Your work and plan in my world. I submit myself to You now, Lord, to forever be a part of the family of God. I thank You for Your plans for me and for the gifts you have given me. Father, please help me to use every gift You give me to be a blessing to others as I serve You. Please teach me to run to You when I mess up or miss the mark. Thank You for forgiving me, loving me, and continually restoring me. I pray in Jesus's name. Amen!

WELCOME

Welcome to the family of God (or welcome back to your rightful place in God)! Please contact me to let me know you joined the family or were restored! God loves you and will never stop! I love you and bless you in Jesus's name!

Affirm Greatness Realize Destiny

Triunity Empowerment Enterprises

C Gaines

7600 Roosevelt Road #129

Forest Park, Illinois 60130

Scripture references on the benefits and inheritance of the family of God (also known as the Body and Bride of Christ):

- Jeremiah 29:11
- Jeremiah 31:3
- John 3:16-17
- John 6:37-40
- John 10:27-30
- Acts 1:8
- Romans 10:9-11
- Romans 10:13
- 2 Corinthians 10:3-5
- Ephesians 5:26-27
- Philippians 4:8
- 1 John 1:9

Meditate on these and get to know God,
or get to know Him better!

Made in the USA
Columbia, SC
07 October 2022

69029807R00083